JOHN McCAIN

OVERCOMING ADVERSITY

JOHN McCAIN

Richard Kozar

Introduction by James Scott Brady,
Trustee, the Center to Prevent Handgun Violence
Vice Chairman, the Brain Injury Foundation

Chelsea House Publishers
Philadelphia

CHELSEA HOUSE PUBLISHERS

EDITOR IN CHIEF Sally Cheney
DIRECTOR OF PRODUCTION Kim Shinners
PRODUCTION MANAGER Pamela Loos
ART DIRECTOR Sara Davis
SENIOR EDITOR John Ziff
PRODUCTION EDITOR Diann Grasse
LAYOUT 21st Century Publishing and Communications, Inc.

First Printing

1 3 5 7 9 8 6 4 2

The Chelsea House World Wide Web address is
http://www.chelseahouse.com

Library of Congress Cataloging-in-Publication Data
Kozar, Richard.
John McCain / Richard Kozar.
p. cm. — (Overcoming adversity)
Includes bibliographical references and index.
ISBN 0-7910-6299-6 (hc : alk. paper) – ISBN 0-7910-6300-3 (pbk. : alk. paper)
1. McCain, John, 1936—Juvenile literature. 2. Literature—United States—Biography—Juvenile literature. 3. United States. Congress. Senate—Biography—Juvenile literature. 4. Prisoners of war—Vietnam—Biography—Juvenile literature. 5. Prisoners of war—United States—Biography—Juvenile literature. 6. United States Naval Academy—Biography—Juvenile literature. [1. McCain, John, 1936- 2. Legislators. 3. Prisoner of war. 4. Presidential candidates.] I. Title. II. Series.

E840.8.M26 K68 2001
328.73'092—dc21

CONTENTS

OVERCOMING ADVERSITY

TIM ALLEN
comedian/performer

MAYA ANGELOU
author

APOLLO 13 MISSION
astronauts

LANCE ARMSTRONG
professional cyclist

DREW BARRYMORE
actress

DREW CAREY
comedian/performer

JIM CARREY
comedian/performer

BILL CLINTON
U.S. president

TOM CRUISE
actor

GAIL DEVERS
Olympian

MICHAEL J. FOX
actor

MOHANDAS K. GANDHI
political/spiritual leader

WHOOPI GOLDBERG
comedian/performer

EKATERINA GORDEEVA
figure skater

SCOTT HAMILTON
figure skater

JEWEL
singer and poet

JAMES EARL JONES
actor

QUINCY JONES
musician and producer

MARIO LEMIEUX
hockey legend

ABRAHAM LINCOLN
U.S. president

JOHN McCAIN
political leader

WILLIAM PENN
Pennsylvania's founder

JACKIE ROBINSON
baseball legend

ROSEANNE
entertainer

MONICA SELES
tennis star

SAMMY SOSA
baseball star

DAVE THOMAS
entrepreneur

SHANIA TWAIN
entertainer

ROBIN WILLIAMS
performer

BRUCE WILLIS
actor

STEVIE WONDER
entertainer

TRIUMPH OF
THE IMAGINATION:
The story of writer
J. K. Rowling

ON FACING ADVERSITY

James Scott Brady

I GUESS IT'S a long way from a Centralia, Illinois, train yard to the George Washington University Hospital Trauma Unit. My dad was a yardmaster for the old Chicago, Burlington & Quincy Railroad. As a child, I used to get to sit in the engineer's lap and imagine what it was like to drive that train. I guess I always have liked being in the "driver's seat."

Years later, however, my interest turned from driving trains to driving campaigns. In 1979, former Texas governor John Connally hired me as a press secretary in his campaign for the American presidency. We lost the Republican primary to a former Hollywood star named Ronald Reagan. But I managed to jump over to the Reagan campaign. When Reagan was elected in 1980, I was "sitting in the catbird seat," as humorist James Thurber would say—poised to be named presidential press secretary. I held that title throughout the eight years of the Reagan administration. But not without one terrible, extended interruption.

It happened barely two months after the Reagan administration took office. I never even heard the shots. On March 30, 1981, my life went blank in an instant. In an attempt to assassinate President Reagan, John Hinckley Jr. armed himself with a "Saturday night special"—a low-quality, $29 pistol—and shot wildly as our presidential entourage exited a Washington hotel. One of the exploding bullets struck me just above the left eye. It shattered into a couple dozen fragments, some of which penetrated my skull and entered my brain.

The next few months of my life were a nightmare of repeated surgery, broken contact with the outside world, and a variety of medical complications. More than once, I was very close to death.

The next few years were filled with frustrating struggles to function with a paralyzed right side, struggles to speak and communicate.

To people who face and defeat daunting obstacles, "ambition" is not becoming wealthy or famous or winning elections or awards. Words like "ambition" and "achievement" and "success" take on very different meanings. The objective is just to live, to wake up every morning. The goals are not lofty; they are very ordinary.

My own heroes are ordinary folks—but they accomplish extraordinary things because they try. My greatest hero is my wife, Sarah. She's accomplished a lot of things in life, but two stand out. The first has been the way she has cared for me and our son since I was shot. A tremendous tragedy and burden was dropped unexpectedly into her life, totally beyond her control and without justification. She could have given up; instead, she focused her energies on preserving our family and returning our lives to normal as much as possible. Week by week, month by month, year by year, she has not reached for the miraculous, just for the normal. Yet in focusing on the normal, she has helped accomplish the miraculous.

Her other most remarkable accomplishment, to me, has been spearheading the effort to keep guns out of the hands of criminals and children in America. Opponents call her a "gun grabber"; I call her a national hero. And I am not alone.

After a seven-year battle, during which Sarah and I worked tirelessly to educate the public about the need for stronger gun laws, the Brady Bill became law in 1993. It was a victory, achieved in the face of tremendous opposition, that now benefits all Americans. From the time the law took effect through fall 1997, background checks had stopped 173,000 criminals and other high-risk purchasers from buying handguns, and the law has helped to reduce illegal gun trafficking.

Sarah was not pursuing fame, or even recognition. She simply started at one point—when our son, Scott, found a loaded handgun on the seat of a pickup truck and, thinking it was a toy, pointed it at Sarah.

Fortunately, no one was hurt. But seeing a gun nearly bring a second tragedy upon our family, Sarah became determined to do whatever she could to prevent senseless death and injury from guns.

Some people think of Sarah as a powerful political force. To me, she's the person who so many times fed me and helped me dress during my long years of recovery.

Overcoming obstacles is part of life, not just for people who are challenged by disabilities, illnesses, or tragedies, but for all people. No matter what the obstacle—fear, disability, prejudice, grief, or a difficulty that isn't likely to "just go away"—we can all work to make this world a better place.

John McCain strikes a "top gun" pose. McCain's extraordinary personal odyssey would begin in the skies over North Vietnam during an ill-fated combat mission.

1

A FIGHTING TRADITION

THERE ARE TWO kinds of war heroes: those who are killed in action, and those who live to fight another day. On October 26, 1967, fate couldn't seem to decide in which category U.S. Navy pilot John McCain belonged.

While he was flying a bombing mission over Hanoi, North Vietnam, with 19 other U.S. pilots, the right wing of his A-4 Skyhawk jet was sheared off by a Russian-made surface-to-air missile (SAM). SAMs were so large they reminded some American pilots of flying telephone poles.

Lieutenant Commander McCain's mortally wounded A-4 began spinning wildly toward the earth. He dodged certain death seconds later by pulling the lever that blew his plane's glass canopy off and simultaneously launched him out of the cockpit. The ejection maneuver is hazardous when a plane is flying upright with both wings intact. McCain's jet was plummeting out of control at hundreds of miles per hour, and his body paid the price.

Fortunately, he barely knew what hit him because he lost consciousness after bailing out. He awoke moments later, having splashed down in a small lake in downtown Hanoi, the capital city of North Vietnam and heart of his enemies' country.

Battered though he was, the 31-year-old flier managed to kick off the muddy lake bottom—15 feet underwater—and struggle to the surface, where he gulped air once or twice before slowly sinking again. Helpless as a newborn because of his injuries, he avoided drowning only by inflating his life jacket.

Vietnamese soldiers towed him ashore, where a mob of civilians had gathered, intent on taking revenge. As they attacked him, he became aware of excruciating pain in his already crippled body.

Then, in one of the rare but remarkable acts of kindness he would witness after being shot down, a woman gave him a sip of tea. And someone in the crowd convinced the others not to kill the American soldier who had just dropped bombs on their city.

McCain was taken to Hoa Lo penitentiary, a compound that many American prisoners of war, or POWs, would be forced to call home for years—if they lived. John McCain himself was at death's door when he was thrown into a cell. His injuries were so severe, in fact, that they might have been life-threatening even had McCain found himself in one of America's finest hospitals. And no one would mistake McCain's quarters for a fine hospital. He was offered little more than bandages and stingy rations of food and water, which he could barely keep in his stomach, during his first terrifying days of imprisonment.

Moreover, because he refused to tell his captors anything more than his name, military rank, and serial number—which is precisely what military personnel are trained to do if captured—they beat him periodically until he blacked out. When he was alert enough to assess his injuries, their severity nearly made him pass out again.

His arms and leg broken, a helpless Lieutenant Commander John McCain is pulled from Truc Bach Lake by North Vietnamese soldiers, October 26, 1967. McCain had been forced to eject after his A-4 Skyhawk jet took a hit from a surface-to-air missile.

McCain pleaded with a guard and the prison's doctor, but they declined to help him because they doubted he would survive. "It's too late, it's too late," the guard said as he and the doctor left.

But several hours later, McCain's heart leapt when another North Vietnamese official walked into his cell and asked whether he was the son of a high-ranking naval officer. "Yes, my father is an admiral," answered the pilot, who instantly realized his captors might consider him worth patching up after all.

Hours later he was lying in bed in a decrepit hospital, undergoing a blood transfusion and other life-sustaining aid. For the moment he appeared to be surviving another brush with death. What McCain couldn't know was just how much more pain, abuse, and heartache he would endure before setting foot again in his beloved United States.

Thirty-three years later, in the year 2000, John McCain was a veteran U.S. senator, his grinning face a familiar sight on magazine covers, newspapers, and television news shows. Most people were vaguely aware the white-haired Arizona lawmaker was a war hero. But that's not why he was making headlines. McCain was undertaking a crusade many school kids have at one point entertained—running for president of the United States. At the age of 63, the feisty former POW displayed the same grit in the presidential race as he had during his hellish captivity decades before.

Of course, running for president isn't a life-or-death race, at least not to most candidates. And early on in the Republican primary season McCain wasn't even expected to seriously challenge his more famous, and better financed, opponents.

But they and the rest of America were about to learn what this war hero's Vietnamese captors had discovered three decades earlier—McCain wasn't an easy man to defeat, and he never backed down from a fight.

■ ■ ■

John Sidney McCain III came from a long line of people who didn't back down from a fight. Men from both branches of his Scotch-Irish family had fought in every U.S. war since the American Revolution, when ancestor Captain John Young served under George Washington. For two centuries this heritage had bestowed a badge of honor. But by John McCain III's generation, it also carried the burden of great expectations. He was expected to follow the path traveled by his father, Admiral John Sidney McCain Jr., who had a generation earlier retraced the steps of his father, Admiral John Sidney McCain Sr.

Thus, John III didn't wind up in the navy so much by choice as by tradition, a tough pill to swallow for a young man who had also inherited his family's rebellious streak.

Three generations of John McCains, 1936. Growing up, the youngest McCain would feel a certain amount of resentment over expectations that he'd follow in the footsteps of his distinguished forebears, who both attained the rank of admiral in the U.S. Navy.

"My life was charted out for me, and I resented that. Not consciously, but clearly subconsciously," he confessed in *Esquire*. "You know, ever since I can remember, as a little boy [I heard]: 'He's going to the Naval Academy.' "

The third John McCain was born in the Panama Canal Zone on August 29, 1936. Three months later, his family packed its bags and followed his father, a submarine commander, to New London, Connecticut. This was just the first in a long line of upheavals for McCain. Until the day John III entered the Naval Academy at age 17, his life would be that of a nomad's. His family never lived in one place long enough to call it home. Moreover, life as a navy "brat" was like life with a single parent.

"We see much less of our fathers than do other children. Our fathers are often at sea, in peace and war," McCain revealed in *Faith of My Fathers*, his 1999 memoir. "Our mothers run our households, pay the bills, and manage most of our upbringing. For long stretches of time they are required to be both mother and father. They move us from base to base. . . . It is no surprise then that the personalities of children who have grown up in the Navy often resemble those of their mothers more than those of their fathers."

McCain's gregarious mother, Roberta, may have indeed fostered his outgoing nature. The daredevil in his personality, however, likely descended directly from grandfather John "Slew" McCain, who distinguished himself in World Wars I and II. But it was as an admiral overseeing the aircraft carrier force of the Third Fleet that McCain Sr. capped his career. In fact, he joined other American brass in accepting Japan's surrender in 1945 on the deck of the USS *Missouri* in Tokyo Bay.

Days afterward, the weary warrior, who had been relieved of his command in the Pacific, collapsed of a heart attack and died at his California home. Condolences poured in from admirals, generals, and President Harry Truman, and his death merited mention on the front page of the *New York Times*.

The eldest McCain left an indelible impression on a grandson who was just shy of nine years old at the time of his passing. Because of his navy responsibilities, Slew, like John's own father, had been an infrequent visitor. But when he did make an appearance his grandchildren were gathered for a photo, even if they had to be rousted from their sleep in the middle of the night. "In pictures of him from the war you sense his irreverent, eccentric individualism," John McCain recalled. "He looked like a

"He looked like a cartoonist's rendering of an old salt," John McCain would write of his grandfather, John "Slew" McCain. "As a young boy and a young man, I found the attitude his image conveyed irresistible."

cartoonist's rendering of an old salt. As a young boy and a young man, I found the attitude his image conveyed irresistible. Perhaps not consciously, I spent much of my youth—and beyond—exaggerating that attitude, too much for my own good, and my family's peace of mind."

Indeed, reckless individualism was a trait—some have said a fault—all three McCains shared in abundance. Another was their academically challenged years at the U.S. Naval Academy at Annapolis, Maryland. Slew McCain, described as a "less than serious student" by his grandson, would graduate in 1906 in the bottom quarter of his class. Still, his modest accomplishment would be the high-water mark for McCain men at the venerable institution.

By 1935, then-Captain McCain tried his hand at flying, a required skill for aspiring aircraft carrier skippers. He may have set a record for death-defying performances, crashing five planes during his training. At one navy base, sailors prayed for his safe return. Yet, at the ripe age of 52, he earned his "wings."

Nothing is more difficult for a son than to live in the shadow of his father's achievements. Yet Slew's son, Jack, carved out his own naval career despite the inevitable comparisons to the old man. And he did so even though he received little hands-on training from the father he was expected to emulate. When the second John Sidney McCain was born in Council Bluffs, Iowa, his dad was predictably absent at sea.

In his memoirs, the youngest McCain recalled how living with high expectations led him to rebel against authority, fight at the drop of a hat, and generally lead a reckless young life. He imagined his father felt much the same way, perhaps because he was forced to enter the Naval Academy while still a spindly teen. "I went in there at the age of sixteen, and I weighed one hundred and five pounds," Admiral Jack McCain told an interviewer decades later. "I could barely carry a Springfield rifle."

Jack's list of shortcomings didn't stop there. His grades were poor from the start and never advanced much in the four years to follow. Nor did his rank in the class, which hovered near the bottom. And then there were the demerits for bad conduct: 114 his first term, almost twice as many the second. The infractions included swearing, fighting, being absent without leave, and showing disrespect toward superiors.

Jack McCain's justification? "Some of these upperclassmen would come up and make some of these statements to you, and required you to do such things which only incited rebellion and mutiny in me," he recalled years later. "And although I did them, the attitude was there, and they didn't like that. But it was a fine institution."

During his senior year, the Naval Academy's administrators threatened to expel the troublemaker and banished him to a rusty warship docked in the nearby harbor where he couldn't corrupt fellow classmates in the dorms. Sensing that he may have pushed the envelope too far, Jack McCain suddenly saw the light. "I shined my shoes and everything else and did everything right. . . . I think that was the closest call I had," he revealed.

Jack McCain had desperately wanted to attend flight school as his father had done, but he couldn't pass the physical. After a brief tour of sea duty on the USS *Oklahoma*, he transferred to the submarine service.

For many Americans in 1941, the "date which will live in infamy" was their call to arms. On the morning of December 7, the Japanese launched a surprise attack on Pearl Harbor, Hawaii, home of America's Pacific Fleet. Within hours, about 2,400 U.S. servicemen caught unawares were dead, more than 1,100 were wounded, and the bottled-up fleet suffered devastating losses. A day later, the United States declared war on Japan. Droves of young men enlisted to defend their country.

Most Americans alive in those days never forgot where they were when they heard about the attack. John McCain III, five at the time, was standing in his New London front yard with his family when a naval officer driving by broke the news to his dad. Like thousands of other American servicemen, the head of the McCain household said his good-byes and raced off to join the war effort. He would be gone for most of the next four years.

He eventually wound up commanding the USS *Gunnel*, a submarine whose crew performed a crucial reconnaissance mission scouting the beaches off North Africa days before an invasion. On the day of the attack, the *Gunnel* served as a beacon, guiding landing craft safely onto the beach. Afterward, McCain and his crew were hounded by

The McCain family, photographed during a rare time when they were all together during World War II. Like most navy wives, Roberta (left) raised her children largely on her own. Rounding out this 1944 portrait are Joe, John, Slew, Sandy, and Jack.

German subs—and, on occasion, friendly aircraft whose pilots mistook the *Gunnel* for a Nazi U-boat. Despite failing engines and a gauntlet of enemy submarines, the Americans managed to slip into safe harbor in England for repairs.

Jack McCain earned a commendation for accomplishing his mission, and it appeared his failure to enter flight school had been a blessing in disguise. For someone who chafed under the close scrutiny of superiors, being a submarine commander was the perfect assignment. Where else could a man make life-or-death decisions on a daily basis without someone looking over his shoulder?

What's more, the shy man who felt uncomfortable in social situations found himself naturally at ease with his officers and enlisted men, who considered "Captain Jack" one of their own. "If you lose the respect of these men, you are finished," he said years later at a commencement address. "You can never get it back."

The *Gunnel* and her crew's next assignment was half a world away in the Pacific, where the U.S. Navy had regrouped after Pearl Harbor and was scouring the seas in search of enemy prey. Near the Korean coast, the sub intercepted a Japanese freight convoy and launched several torpedoes that sank two ships. Enemy escort vessels immediately began stalking the sub, dropping depth charges that rattled the *Gunnel's* steel hull and its crew.

After a deadly game of cat-and-mouse, McCain managed to send another Japanese vessel—this one a prowling destroyer—to the bottom. Despite additional pounding from depth charges, he and his men hid out in the ocean depths until they had barely enough oxygen and battery power remaining to surface. Instead of the artillery shelling they expected to encounter topside, they were relieved to see the remaining destroyers steaming off in the distance. Grateful, the men aboard the *Gunnel* swung her in the opposite direction and limped away.

In recognition of his cool under fire, Jack McCain was awarded the Silver Star. And at the war's conclusion in 1945, he sailed the submarine USS *Dentuda* into Tokyo Bay, where he and Admiral Slew McCain briefly swapped war stories and renewed their father-son relationship. Neither knew it would be for the last time.

In some ways, the son would surpass the father. Not only did Jack ultimately become a four-star admiral (Slew received his fourth star posthumously), but he was also named Commander in Chief, Pacific Command (CINCPAC). It was a coveted post, considered in some quarters the ultimate navy assignment. The person who held it commanded U.S. forces in the Pacific from the tip of Alaska to Antarctica, from California to Southeast Asia. And in 1968, that meant the CINCPAC also oversaw the war in Vietnam.

McCain, cigar in mouth and seated behind the wheel of a sports car, poses with his roommate Frank Gamboa the day before his graduation from the U.S. Naval Academy. Rebellious and defiant, the young midshipman had come within a hairbreadth of being expelled from Annapolis.

2

REBEL WITHOUT A CAUSE

WHILE JOHN McCAIN'S father was climbing the U.S. Navy's promotion ladder, his mother was doing her best to raise their three children, Sandy, John, and Joe. Although it's not known outside the McCain family who was the most precocious of the three, John has certainly acquired quite a reputation in the press. When he didn't get his way as a toddler, he held his breath until he passed out. Once, on a lengthy road trip with his brother and sister, his mother hit him with an aluminum thermos after one too many wisecracks. Joe would later observe: "John was either fiercely immersed in the squabble or the root cause of it."

McCain was short, which didn't improve his nature, especially when he had to adjust to each new school the children were forced to attend on every new navy base. Eager to prove he could hold his ground, he resorted to fighting at the first sign of a challenge. Whether he had cause or not, John McCain was as determined as his forefathers to be his own man—and damn the consequences.

The McCain children shuffled from base to base, and school to school, making friendships the hard way and enduring the inevitable heartaches when they ended. In the midst of this transient lifestyle, young John developed an iron self-reliance—and a distaste for authority from which he may never have fully recovered. He particularly resented being picked on simply because he was the new kid in town or a member of the youngest class in a school. "At each new school I grew more determined to assert my crude individualism," he wrote. "At each new school I became a more unrepentant pain in the neck."

When he began attending the all-male Episcopal High School in Alexandria, Virginia—a gracious Southern institution that typically prepared its upper-class teens for college and respectable careers—he found the perfect training ground for his crude individualism. Episcopal was a disciplined prep school, not a summer camp. Its regimen included tough academics and sports, a dress code, and demerits, those nettlesome punishments for breaking the rules.

The only military-bound student, John McCain accumulated demerits like overachievers earned extra credit. His room was a pigsty, he showed up for class when it suited him, and he resisted tooth and nail the hazing inflicted on him and other first-year students. "Like the Virginia Military Institute and the Citadel, Episcopal imposed on first-year students the designation 'rats,'" he recalled in his book. "Rats were expected to submit to a comparatively mild form of hazing. Mild or not, I resented the hell out of it." He soon became known as the "worst rat."

In the best McCain tradition, his grades were uneven, which he justified by pointing out that he excelled in subjects that intrigued him, such as English and history. Nonetheless, he graduated in 1954. Unlike his high school chums, who had a summer off before college, he

was driven by his father through the gates of the Naval Academy in June for the start of "plebe summer." (At Annapolis a plebe is a first-year student.)

Early on, McCain decided the Naval Academy wasn't so bad after all. He likened it to a camp where a bunch of guys wrestled, boxed, and marched in step.

McCain (seated, third from right) with teammates from Episcopal Academy. The future senator "resented the hell out of" the hazing he received as a freshman at the elite prep school.

Even the supervising upperclassmen didn't seem so bad . . . at first.

However, plebe summer was the calm before the storm for first-year students. When Labor Day passed and the upper three classes of midshipmen (students at the Naval Academy) returned, plebe life changed dramatically—for the worse. Like his fellow plebes, John McCain soon discovered that Annapolis was no different from the countless other schools he had attended in his rambling youth. Upperclassmen not only ruled, they made the new kids on the block sorry they had ever been born.

In those days, hazing was a traditional but miserable fact of life for plebes, the navy's way of toughening those future officers who could survive it and weeding out those who would never have the right stuff. By the end of John McCain's four years at the Naval Academy, 25 percent of his classmates had dropped out. Based on the admissions of those who graduated, nearly everyone else considered doing so at least once. McCain's younger brother, Joe, washed out of Annapolis as a plebe in 1961.

The Naval Academy's time-honored approach was simple: break midshipmen down until their individuality ceased to exist, and then remake them into leaders whom men would follow into combat. The indignities of plebe life began with crew cuts and ended wherever upperclassmen drew the line. Some plebes were ruthlessly paddled by upperclassmen for minor infractions, even though the practice was technically prohibited. The strongest victims gritted their teeth in silence only to retreat to their rooms and cry themselves to sleep. Writer and former midshipmen Robert Timberg, author of *The Nightingale's Song,* summed up plebe year this way: "If anything, the upper-class seemed intent on driving you out. Their ridiculous and demeaning demands consumed every free moment. When they weren't hazing you physically, they were ordering you to find the answers to mindless questions that left no time to study for class." A typical request, he noted, would be to find out "the name of the lead elephant in Hannibal's caravan when the Carthaginians crossed the Alps to invade Italy."

How did John McCain survive plebe year? Just as he had every other institution that ranked newcomers as the lowest of the low. His shoes and belt buckle weren't the shiniest, and his uniform wasn't the most crisp. He tolerated the habitual abuse—just barely—and remained defiant toward those who were in power simply because they were older. Finally, he flaunted rules as if he were duty-bound to try to break them. One night his rowdy gang scaled the Naval Academy walls and made its way to a ramshackle bar seven miles away that was off-limits. When military police raided the bar, McCain and his drinking buddies scattered like rats deserting a sinking ship.

His antics had indeed attracted a following, and not just of fellow misfits. Otherwise-conscientious plebes seemed to enjoy hanging out with a bad boy, eager to live on the wild side occasionally. McCain was proving he could inspire men just as well as those spit-and-polish plebes at the top of his class. He was a rebel without a cause, but he was also turning out to be a leader despite his low opinion of the Naval Academy's hallowed traditions.

Like his father, McCain came perilously close to being booted out of Annapolis altogether his final year, when his demerit count soared to just shy of the maximum required for expulsion. He was fed up with a system that he felt punished capable men for no reason other than it had always been so. He was also under attack by a captain who had made it his mission to expel the irreverent midshipman.

Despite the captain's scrutiny, McCain squeaked

Though he chafed at some of the Naval Academy's traditions and regulations, McCain, ever the fighter, battled the system through to graduation. Here he is seen in a different fight, as a Naval Academy boxer.

through and graduated with his class in the spring of 1958. His rank: fifth from the bottom.

McCain would look back on his years at Annapolis with a mixture of fondness and indignation, but he eventually realized his ordeals there toughened him for far more severe tests down the road. There were other insights as well. "The most important lesson I learned there was that to sustain my self-respect for a lifetime it would be necessary for me to have the honor of serving something greater than my self-interest," he wrote.

Navy pilot John McCain (first row, second from left) with members of his fighter squadron on board the USS Intrepid, *1963.*

3

THE SKY'S THE LIMIT

AFTER GRADUATING FROM the U.S. Naval Academy, John McCain III decided to accomplish what his father had been unable to do: become a navy pilot. He passed the required physical and began flight training.

Initially, however, McCain the aviator resembled McCain the midshipman. He was a so-so flier, just as he'd been a mediocre student. Yet he had no trouble assuming the characteristic swagger of a navy "top gun"—driving fast cars, dating fast women, and living life as if it were one big party.

Like his crash-prone aviator grandfather, Slew McCain, John had a brush with death during his flight school days. He was practicing landings on a runway overlooking Corpus Christi Bay in Texas when his engine suddenly stalled. The last thing he remembers is slamming into the waves.

He came to underwater and squeezed out of his plane with just enough air left in his lungs to claw back to the surface.

Doctors later determined he hadn't broken any bones or sustained internal injuries. In fact, after taking painkillers and resting, the carefree flyboy rallied later that evening for another night of revelry. It was hard to keep McCain down.

Later in his training in the early 1960s, which had advanced to takeoffs and landings aboard aircraft carriers, McCain began to enjoy flying, as well as tours of duty at sea. He even earned the designation of "officer of the deck underway," signifying that he was qualified to navigate a ship. Whether because he'd begun to mature or simply because of the absence of onshore temptations, McCain's thoughts turned from mischief to continuing an honorable family tradition. "I had, by this time, begun to aspire to command. I didn't possess any particular notion of greatness, but I did hold strong notions of honor," he reflected in *Faith of My Fathers*. "And I worried that my deserved reputation for foolishness would make command of a squadron or a carrier, the pinnacle of a young pilot's aspiration, too grand an ambition for an obstreperous admiral's son, and my failure to reach command would dishonor me and my family."

His superiors couldn't help noticing his gradual improvement, which was marred only by the occasional stunt. On one occasion, for example, he caused a blackout in southern Spain after flying so low his jet severed power lines.

Once back in the states, McCain became a flight instructor at a sleepy airbase in Meridian, Mississippi, where he would later be named instructor of the month. He was also gaining renown for his ability to inject excitement into the most boring surroundings. He and his bachelor buddies had transformed a mosquito-infested lakeside next to their barracks into a popular watering hole known as the Key Fess Yacht Club. Navy fliers throughout the country in those years considered Meridian a must-see.

Carol Shepp, a divorced mother of two, wed John McCain on July 3, 1965.

But John McCain's carefree days were winding down. In July 1965, he married former model Carol Shepp, a divorced mother of two he had known at the Naval Academy. At age 28, he quietly settled down and adopted her two young boys. He and Carol also became the proud parents of a daughter, Sydney, a little over a year later.

His family's military pedigree loomed larger and larger in his mind, especially after another plane crash. He was flying back from a December Army-Navy football game in Philadelphia, Pennsylvania, en route to Norfolk, Virginia, for refueling, when his trainer plane lost power over Virginia's uninhabited shoreline. He ejected 1,000 feet above the marshy terrain and parachuted to safety as his plane, loaded with Christmas presents for his children, crashed into a grove of trees. Escaping with only scratches and bruises, he was rescued by a military helicopter minutes later.

Still, the incident reinforced his understanding of the fine line between life and death, which a military pilot treads daily. In his book, he said, "This latest unexpected glimpse of mortality added even greater urgency to my recent existential inquiries and made me all the more anxious to get to Vietnam before some new unforeseen accident prevented me from ever taking my turn in war."

Being a McCain meant proving oneself in combat, and in 1967 the proving ground was Vietnam. Since the mid-1950s the United States had been involved in the affairs of this Southeast Asian land, which, after successfully rebelling against French colonial rule, had been divided into Communist North Vietnam and non-Communist South Vietnam. Planned elections to unify the country were never held, and tensions between the two sides eventually erupted into fighting. Initially the U.S. military played a largely advisory role in assisting South Vietnam. But gradually the United States began taking a more active role in the conflict, and by the mid-1960s hundreds of thousands of American soldiers and airmen were fighting alongside America's South Vietnamese allies. North Vietnam, on the other hand, was being aided by the Soviet Union and Communist China.

John McCain joined a squadron aboard the carrier USS *Forrestal,* where he would complete his bomber training in the A-4 Skyhawk. Eventually, the *Forrestal* and her crew completed the voyage to Southeast Asia and cruised the waters of the South China Sea less than 100 miles from North Vietnam. This particular location in the Tonkin Gulf was known as Yankee Station.

Flying combat missions from an aircraft carrier requires nerves of steel and abundant skill. A carrier's landing deck is much smaller than an airport runway, but the hazards of putting the plane down safely are greatly surpassed by the dangers of flying a mission in the face of enemy fire. The best navy fliers seem to have equal amounts of bravado and talent, along with a craving for adrenaline that is best quenched by shooting and being shot at.

Like baseball players convinced they must dress for a game exactly the same way each day to preserve a hitting streak, combat pilots are often a superstitious lot. John McCain had his own preflight ritual aboard the *Forrestal*. By July 29, 1967, he had five successful bombing missions under his belt, and he wasn't anxious to break the young streak in its infancy. As he waited his turn to take off that day, his routine concluded with having his helmet's visor cleaned by his parachute rigger, a pilot's eyes and ears on the flight deck. McCain's A-4 Skyhawk was third in line on the port, or left, side of the *Forrestal,* nose facing the front of the massive carrier. Opposite him on the starboard, or right, side were rows of F-4s, the fighter jets armed with air-to-ground Zuni rockets and machine guns to protect the bombers during their mission.

The typical mission took less than an hour from start to finish. "Combat for a naval aviator is fought in short, violent bursts. . . . We are spared the sustained misery of the infantrymen who slog through awful conditions and danger for months on end," McCain noted.

On this day, however, no mission would be flown. His rigger, Tom Ott, had barely given McCain the traditional thumbs-up before takeoff when the unimaginable happened: a Zuni rocket on a nearby F-4 was accidentally launched by a faulty electrical charge. The errant six-foot missile pierced McCain's detachable belly fuel tank and unleashed 200 gallons of flaming fuel onto the flight deck. Two of his A-4's 1,000-pound bombs had also been dislodged and were now simmering in the liquid inferno.

McCain flung open his glass canopy, scrambled down the jet's nose and spearlike refueling probe, and leaped into a wall of fire. His flight suit caught fire, but he managed to put out the flames while running for the starboard side of the carrier. Meanwhile, enlisted men and officers alike grabbed extinguishers and hoses to douse the blaze as a dazed McCain watched.

The pilot in the A-4 next to him was engulfed in fire after fleeing his jet. As McCain moved to help him, one of the bombs from his jet exploded, hurling metal fragments into his legs and chest and knocking him over backwards. His nearest shipmates were less fortunate; his rigger, the burning pilot, and a chief petty officer trying to extinguish the blaze were killed instantly.

A carrier commander's worst nightmare was unfolding before the crew's eyes. Plane after plane caught fire and blew up, adding fuel and explosive power to the carnage. Additional Zuni missiles launched though no one had fired them. Trapped pilots took their chances by jumping or ejecting into the inferno, which had now spread through the cratered three-and-a-half-inch flight deck to the hangar deck below. McCain recalls pieces of metal and human flesh falling from the sky onto the burning deck around him.

Although wounded, he insisted on helping other men move bombs stored on the hangar deck before the blaze ignited them. Afterward, in an area of the ship away from the fire, he joined his fellow pilots who were numbly watching the tragedy unfold via closed-circuit television screens.

"The fires were consuming the *Forrestal*. I thought she might sink," McCain wrote in *Faith of My Fathers*. "But the crew's heroics kept her afloat. Men sacrificed their lives for one another and for their

Sailors scramble to clear munitions from the burning deck of the carrier Forrestal, *July 29, 1967. The deadly incident began when a rocket from a fighter jet accidentally fired into McCain's bomber as the planes were waiting to take off for a mission. McCain was lucky to escape with his life; 134 of his crewmates weren't so fortunate.*

ship. Many of them were only eighteen and nineteen years old. They fought the inferno with tenacity usually reserved for hand-to-hand combat. They fought it all day and well into the next, and they saved the *Forrestal*."

In all, 134 men were accounted dead or missing, including a few who had jumped overboard to escape certain death on the flight deck. In the first five minutes of the accident, nine explosions had rocked the carrier, whose skipper at one point considered ordering the crew to abandon ship. The flight deck fire was put out later that first afternoon. It took another day to extinguish the blaze belowdecks. The damage tally, not including 20 destroyed warplanes, came to $72 million. Still afloat, the *Forrestal* sailed slowly to the Philippines for emergency repairs. Eventually she was sent stateside for two years of extensive overhauls.

With the *Forrestal* out of commission indefinitely, McCain fully expected his combat career to be in dry dock as well, a troubling prospect for a warrior who still felt he had much to prove. "As the crippled *Forrestal* limped toward port, my moment was disappearing when it had barely begun, and I feared my ambitions were among the casualties in the calamity that had claimed the *Forrestal*," he said.

His proverbial ship came in, however. Shortly thereafter, an officer from the carrier USS *Oriskany* asked if any *Forrestal* pilots were willing to fill the depleted ranks of combat pilots aboard his ship, which was also launching missions in the Tonkin Gulf. Seizing the day, McCain volunteered, even though the *Oriskany* had suffered its own grim misfortune. Forty-four of its crew had died in a freak fire, and dozens of pilots had been shot down in missions over Vietnam. By 1968, a total of 38 *Oriskany* pilots would be killed or captured.

Despite his new ship's reputation among navy pilots as being "a dangerous place to live," 31-year-old Lieutenant Commander John S. McCain was anxious to climb back into the cockpit. "I was relieved," he recalled, "at this unexpected change in my fortunes."

A North Vietnamese fighter stands over the wreckage of Lieutenant Commander John McCain's Skyhawk. For McCain, the downing of his bomber over Hanoi on October 26, 1967, signaled the beginning of a five-and-a-half-year ordeal.

4

IN HARM'S WAY

JOHN McCAIN WASN'T a particularly religious man, but he must have wondered whether God kept sparing his life for a reason. He had survived two plane crashes as well as the raging inferno aboard the *Forrestal*. No one would have blamed him for thinking twice before strapping himself back into a jet and flying more combat missions.

Especially since North Vietnam's superpower ally, the Soviet Union, was providing a continuous stream of modern weapons and supplies, and American fighting men could do nothing about it. Those running the U.S. war effort, including President Lyndon B. Johnson and Secretary of Defense Robert S. McNamara, were wary of taking any action that might provoke the Soviet Union (or for that matter China) into a wider conflict. Their reasoning was simple: the Soviet Union, like the United States, had a huge nuclear arsenal, and a direct military confrontation could lead to annihilation for both nations. So the goal of U.S. participation in the Vietnam War—checking the spread of communism in Southeast Asia—had to be pursued within strict limitations.

In the opinion of many American military leaders and soldiers actually waging the war, however, the strategy amounted to fighting with one arm tied behind your back. The "rules of engagement" prevented them from striking at targets they deemed vital, such as Russian supply ships unloading surface-to-air missiles in Haiphong Harbor. Those SAMs were being launched from sites surrounding cities like Hanoi, and yet for years pilots couldn't attack those installations either.

"In all candor, we thought our civilian commanders were complete idiots who didn't have the least notion of what it took to win the war," McCain reflected after Vietnam. "I found no evidence in postwar studies of the Johnson administration's political and military decision-making during the war that caused me to revise that harsh judgment."

Some U.S. commanders recognized that as long as America permitted Soviet aid to reach the North Vietnamese unmolested, the best the United States could hope for was a stalemate, and the worst a defeat. Meanwhile, American infantrymen and pilots were dying while politicians back in Washington were micromanaging the war.

Under pressure, President Johnson finally decided to escalate U.S. involvement. *Oriskany* pilots began working 12-hour shifts, with half a day of rest between bombing missions. Few complained, however, particularly John McCain. "For the first time we believed we were helping to win the war, and we were proud to be usefully employed," he recalled. Previously forbidden targets, such as Soviet MiG fighter jets parked on airfields and a thermal power plant in downtown Hanoi, were suddenly fair game.

On October 26, 1967, John McCain was scheduled to

The view from the air the day John McCain was shot down. His target, a power plant, lies on the right side of the lake, just above the bridge. Because fellow pilots saw the flaming wreckage of his plane but didn't see a parachute, McCain was initially assumed to be dead.

join a mission to bomb the power plant. As he walked out of the briefing room, McCain remembers receiving this piece of advice from the carrier's strike operations officer: "You'd better be careful. We're probably going to lose someone on this one." McCain, who was feeling cocky after obliterating two MiGs sitting on an airfield the previous day, told him not to worry.

He was confident in himself and his A-4 Skyhawk, which had been outfitted with the latest technological defense measures, most notably systems that could detect radar tracking from SAM launching sites. The countermeasures alerted pilots to danger by sounding tones in the cockpit. One signified radar tracking; another, radar locked; and the third, missile launched. That day, the attacking U.S. squadron heard the radar-tracking tone miles before they even reached the heavily fortified city limits.

By the time they streaked over Hanoi, alarms were ringing in their ears and the skies were filled with anti-aircraft flak. Before the attack was finished, 22 SAM missiles would add to the mayhem. "We were now maneuvering through a nearly impassable obstacle course of antiaircraft fire and flying telephone poles," McCain would recall. "They scared the hell out of me."

As he dove in for his bombing run, the third ominous tone—indicating a missile coming his way—sounded in the navy flier's cockpit. He had the option of pulling out of the dive and evading the SAM in his highly maneuverable A-4, but he rolled the dice and released his bombs first. He dropped them from 3,500 feet above the power plant, only then pulling back hard on the stick to propel his jet skyward and hopefully to safety. But his luck abruptly ran out. The SAM homing in on his jet blew off the plane's right wing, sending the crippled aircraft into a spin toward earth at 500 miles per hour.

Even then McCain didn't panic, managing to blurt over the radio "I'm hit!" before reaching for the ejection lever. The maneuver spared his life. But as he rocketed out of the cockpit, his flailing arms snapped like kite supports in a hurricane, as did his knee. He passed out while parachuting toward Truc Bach Lake in central Hanoi. It was midday and he had just dropped bombs on the city's power plant, hardly an act destined to earn him much sympathy on the ground.

But first he had to survive the watery landing. Weighted down by his gear, McCain sank like a rock. He managed to kick off the lake bottom and swim to the surface, but he quickly sank again. After realizing his arms were useless, he grasped the toggle of his inflatable life vest between his teeth and pulled it with all his might. He finally surfaced but once again slipped into unconsciousness.

He was soon pulled to shore by Vietnamese soldiers, only to be set upon by a mob of angry villagers, who tore off his clothes, bayoneted his ankle and groin, and bashed his shoulder with a rifle. A woman in the crowd intervened on his behalf, however, first by calming the crowd and then applying crude splints to his leg and one arm.

Afterward, soldiers placed him on a stretcher and drove him several blocks to Hoa Lo Prison, a jail built by the French but now known to American POWs as "the Hanoi Hilton." When the truck pulled into the stone compound, McCain remembers feeling absolute despair. "As the massive steel doors loudly clanked shut behind me, I felt a deeper dread than I have ever felt since."

He would spend the next several days, now fully aware of his painful injuries, lying in his own filth on a stretcher, drifting in and out of consciousness. While he was awake, he was asked for military details that his captors could use against their enemy, such as which targets were likely to be struck in the future. McCain refused to talk.

Because of his injuries he had to be fed by a guard, but eating did little good because he couldn't keep food in his stomach. He was growing weaker by the day and realized that his injuries—particularly his mangled right leg—might soon kill him. He tried bargaining with his captors by promising them anything they wished in return for medical treatment, but even the prison medic didn't see the point after assessing his injuries.

That might have been the end of McCain had not the Vietnamese discovered who his father was. The camp

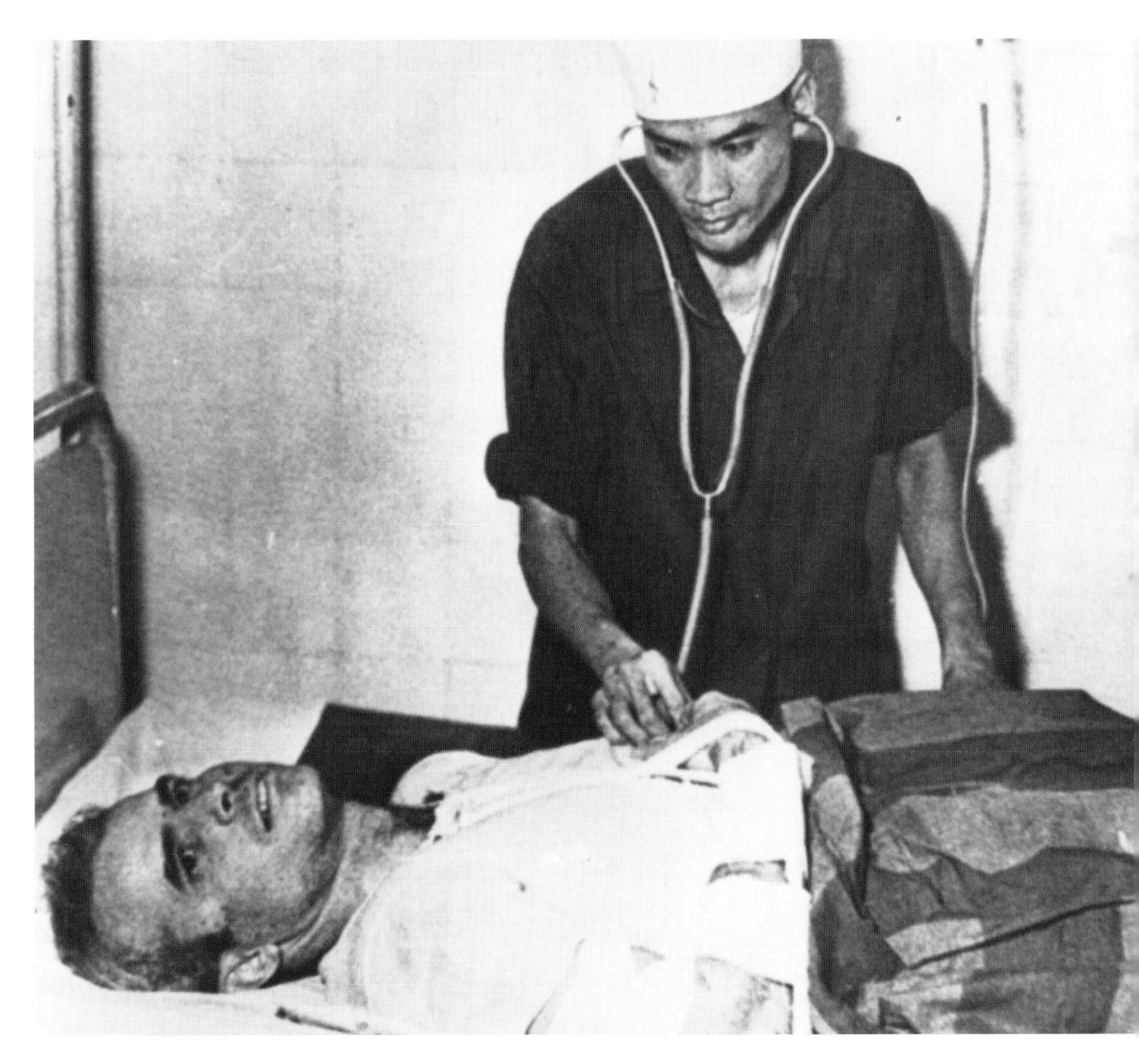

McCain probably would have died in the Hoa Lo Prison, known among American POWs as "the Hanoi Hilton," had the North Vietnamese not discovered that his father was an admiral and transferred him to a hospital. In this photo he is being examined at that hospital.

officer, a half-blind man the prisoners hated and nicknamed Bug, broke the welcome news to the battered navy pilot. "Your father is a big admiral. Now we take you to the hospital."

Although he was transported to a hospital, it was the height of the rainy season, and rats, mosquitoes, and roaches infested the wretched facility. He received blood transfusions and was given nourishment through an intravenous line, but no one treated his broken limbs or even bathed him. Nonetheless, he gradually regained some strength and spent more time awake than unconscious.

His captors took advantage of his alertness to interrogate him periodically, resorting to beatings that McCain learned to shorten by screaming wildly as soon as they commenced. He suspected that the Vietnamese backed off because of his father's rank, and it turned out he was mostly right. Other POWs were brutalized during their first days of incarceration, injured or not, he later learned.

Back in the United States, his family had initially given him up for dead. His fellow pilots had observed the burning wreckage of his jet, but none had seen him bail out.

However, the North Vietnamese, eager to use the downed pilot as a bargaining chip, announced his capture a week later. They even allowed a French journalist to interview McCain. Now determined to display themselves in the best light, the North Vietnamese took a second look at their prisoner's wounds. The best they could do, however, was transfer him to a more sanitary room and slap his upper body and right arm in a plaster cast, which was useless medically but gave the appearance that he was receiving proper care.

McCain reluctantly agreed to the filmed interview, but he offered only the barest details of his capture and subsequent treatment. Asked by the reporter what message he would like to send to his loved ones, he replied, "I would just like to tell my wife that I'm going to get well. I love her, and hope to see her soon. I'd appreciate it if you'd tell her that. That's all I have to say." His captors, expecting a public confession for his "sins," were indignant.

In the days that followed, the North Vietnamese threatened to withhold surgery on his leg if he didn't denounce American involvement in Vietnam. He refused, but ultimately underwent surgery on the injured knee anyway, though the procedure did little good. To this day the ligaments on the right side of his knee serve no function, and he can practically predict approaching bad weather by gauging the degree of pain in his joint.

When he was discharged after six weeks in the hospital, McCain resembled a survivor from a World War II concentration camp. Feverish and gaunt, he had the sunken eyes of someone not long for this world. He had lost 50 pounds while supposedly recuperating from his wounds. Vietnamese officials implied that it was his fault he wasn't getting better, to which he responded, "Put me with other Americans, and I'll get better."

He ended up sharing a cell in a small Hanoi prison with two air force officers, Majors George "Bud" Day and Norris Overly, whom he credits with nursing him back to health. From their perspective, however, the trio's time together began more as a deathwatch. Day knew from personal experience how close his new roommate was to dying. After a harrowing escape from prison earlier that year, he was recaptured within sight of an American helicopter base, then brutally tortured until his arms hung like a rag doll's. He had Overly to thank for bringing him back from the brink of death. "I've seen some dead that looked at least as good as John," Day remembered thinking when he saw McCain hauled in on a stretcher. He added, "I said, 'The [North Vietnamese] have dumped this guy on us so they can blame us for killing him,' because I didn't think he was going to live out the day."

But the stubborn navy pilot refused to die. So like tender parents, Day and Overly cleaned McCain, spoon-fed him, and listened as their patient babbled about his experiences and grilled them about theirs. "I can remember thinking that night, 'My God, this guy's got a lot of heart,'" Day related in *The Nightingale's Song.* "You've been involved in sports and games and things where people kind of rise to an occasion and that was him. He was rising. And if he hadn't been, he'd have been dead. If he had not had that will to live and that determination, he'd have been dead."

An American prisoner of war has a word with fellow captives at a Hanoi POW camp. Enduring the hellish conditions in the camps, including physical and psychological torture, pushed even the most resolute of fighting men to the brink.

5

A LIVING HELL

THANKS PRIMARILY TO Norris Overly, who was in better physical shape than Day, John McCain's condition improved rapidly. Instead of sleeping nearly around the clock, he began to spend more hours awake. Overly washed away the weeks of accumulated grime, scrubbed his patient's infected knee with soap and water, and got him standing on his own two feet by the end of their first week together.

Day, McCain, and Overly received relatively good treatment in their current jail, which had been dubbed "the Plantation." Day in particular suspected that camp officials had ulterior motives for going easy on most prisoners, and his instincts proved correct. It turned out that the Vietnamese intended to release certain POWs, such as McCain, early and thus break the spirit of the other prisoners, almost all of whom had been in captivity longer. However, by accepting such offers an American serviceman would be violating the Code of Conduct of Prisoners of War. The rules stipulated that a POW refuse to accept special treatment from the enemy, plan and carry out escapes wherever practical, and agree to release only after those captured earlier had been set free.

Once McCain realized the Vietnamese were using him as a pawn to embarrass his father and dishearten fellow POWs, he dug in his heels and refused preferential treatment, even the promise of better food. On the other hand, Overly—for reasons that aren't quite clear—decided to accept an early release when his captors offered. He denied having done anything dishonorable in exchange for being set free. McCain took him at his word and refused to condemn his cellmate, to whom he owed his life. Other prisoners were not so charitable. They considered Overly's decision a breach of the Code of Conduct, and labeled the system the "Fink Release Program," noted Robert Timberg in *The Nightingale's Song.*

Bud Day and John McCain managed the best they could without Overly hovering over them. With McCain hobbling around on a pair of decrepit crutches, they helped each other walk and eat, and even scrubbed each other's backs.

The Vietnamese persisted in trying to convince the admiral's son to condemn President Johnson and the American war effort, and to accept an early release. One day, McCain had had enough. He told a contingent of visiting North Vietnamese officials where to go in no uncertain terms.

"It was some of the most colorful profanity that you would ever hope to hear," recalled fellow inmate Jack Van Loan:

> He was calling them every name in the book, and telling them that he was not going home early, that he wasn't going to ask for amnesty and not to ask him that again and to get out and, furthermore, screw you and the horse you rode in on. . . .They would have lugged him out of there that day and let him go. And here's a guy that's all crippled up, all busted up, and he doesn't know if he's going to live to the next day and he literally blew them out of there with a verbal assault. You can't imagine the example John set for the rest of the camp by doing that.

Day and McCain were separated after being confined together for 45 days. For McCain, it marked the beginning of two years of solitary confinement—a grueling test of his character, courage, and sanity. "I cannot adequately describe how sorry I was to part company with my friend and inspiration," McCain said. "Up until then, I don't believe I had ever relied on any other person for emotional and physical support to the extent I had relied on Bud."

In the spring of 1968, Day was transferred to another jail called "the Zoo," a human hellhole where his will to survive would be put to the test. Meanwhile, McCain was moved to a cellblock known as "the Warehouse." He was little more than a shell of his former self. Because of the filthy living conditions in the camp, he had contracted dysentery, a chronic inflammation of the lower intestine that prevents the body from absorbing nutrients. His broken arms served as passable crutch supports, but little else. Then there was the loneliness.

"It's an awful thing, solitary," McCain wrote. "It crushes your spirit and weakens your resistance more effectively than any other form of mistreatment. Having no one else to rely on, to share confidences with, to seek counsel from, you begin to doubt your judgment and your courage." Still, he added, "you eventually adjust to solitary, as you can do to almost any hardship, by devising various methods to keep your mind off your troubles and greedily grasping any opportunity for human contact."

POWs fought off despair by exercising their minds as well as their bodies. Some designed complete houses in their heads; others memorized the name and rank of every prisoner they came in contact with, a tally numbering in the hundreds. And many, including John McCain, turned to prayer for solace. Anything that kept their minds occupied was a welcome relief to staring at four stark walls.

His adversarial nature came in handy as well. For once, the rebel had a cause—irritating his North Vietnamese captors any way he could. As always, he vigorously rejected their offers of early freedom. But it was his bla-

John McCain's POW photo. The aviator's continual displays of defiance and disrespect toward his captors frequently landed him in solitary confinement but buoyed the spirits of his comrades.

tant disrespect for his captors that tickled his fellow prisoners and brought him satisfaction. While being escorted to interrogation sessions, he cursed his handlers up one side and down the other, much to the delight of other POWs watching his antics through cracks in their cell doors. "Solitary also put me in a pretty surly mood, and I would resist depression by hollering insults at my guards, resorting to the belligerence that I had relied on earlier in my life when obliged to suffer one indignity or another," he wrote. "Resisting, being uncooperative and a general pain in the ass, proved, as it had in the past, to be a morale booster for me."

His defiance was tolerated by some, but not all, of the guards. When they felt particularly provoked, they would kick or punch him without hesitation. Still, McCain always felt that the Vietnamese treated him differently—gentler in some ways—than they treated his fellow POWs. If so, that preferential treatment ended in July 1968 when he adamantly refused a repeated offer to go home ahead of fellow POWs.

This time he had been tempted to accept, believing the Code of Conduct made exceptions for severely injured POWs, which he certainly was. "I wanted to say yes. I badly wanted to go home," he confessed in his book. "I was tired and sick, and despite my bad attitude, I was often afraid."

John McCain couldn't know it at the time, but his father was soon to be promoted to CINCPAC, a move the Vietnamese desperately wanted to counter with the potentially embarrassing release of his son.

He agonized over what to do. "I knew that every prisoner the Vietnamese tried to break, those who had arrived before me and those who would come after me, would be taunted with the story of how an admiral's son had gone home early, a lucky beneficiary of America's class-conscious society. . . . I couldn't persuade myself to leave."

He gave camp officials his final no on July 4, 1968, the same day his father became CINCPAC. Then he sat in his cell for nearly two months waiting for retribution. It came when his captors demanded he sign a confession admitting to his "crimes." Their persuasion techniques included tying his arms so tightly behind his back that his shoulder blades practically touched. For several days, he was periodically beaten, losing several teeth in the process. His ribs were cracked and his left arm rebroken.

After four days, McCain knew he was at the end of his rope. Despondent, he made a feeble attempt to hang himself with his shirt before being stopped by a guard. For nearly half a day he argued back and forth with an interrogator determined to obtain a signed confession. In the end, the North Vietnamese got their wish and McCain signed, but the document was mainly one of their own authorship. It read that McCain was a "black criminal" who had "performed deeds of an air pirate" but was nonetheless saved by the Vietnamese people.

Although John McCain didn't realize it then, he was hardly the first POW to crack under torture. Several of the most decorated POWs of the war later revealed they had suffered similar fates. But when it happened to him, and for years afterward, he could not forgive himself even as he would forgive others. "I'm convinced that I did the best that I could," he told Timberg, "but the best that I could wasn't good enough."

In his book, McCain was even more critical. "I couldn't rationalize away my confession. I was ashamed. I felt faithless, and couldn't control my despair. I shook, as if my disgrace were a fever. I kept imagining that they would release my confession to embarrass my father. All my pride was lost, and I doubted I would ever stand up to any man again. Nothing could save me. No one would ever look upon me again with anything but pity and contempt."

He was wrong, of course, but it would take him years to come to terms with his moment of weakness. However, he also learned one of the greatest lessons of his life during those dark times in captivity, he has said. "I discovered in prison that faith in myself alone, separate from other, more important allegiances, was ultimately no match for the cruelty that human beings could devise."

John McCain also realized that a POW's greatest asset was fellow POWs, who could be relied on when one's own fortitude was nearly sapped. To that end, prisoners went to extraordinary lengths to communicate with one another, talking through drinking cups placed against cell walls or tapping code from cell to cell. And should two POWs ever be placed in the same cell together, especially if they had been in solitary, McCain joked that the grateful pair would

Admiral Jack McCain mingles with American troops in South Vietnam, Christmas 1970. After his father's promotion to CINCPAC, John McCain's captors redoubled their efforts to get him to accept early release and thereby embarrass the U.S. military.

jabber incessantly for hours—although neither was probably listening to a word the other said.

Camp inmates had other diversions as well to boost their morale, especially when the North Vietnamese let their guard down in later years. Some became "professors," instructing fellow POWs in whichever discipline they had mastered. At a jail known as Camp Unity, McCain and another prisoner taught history and English literature, two of the few subjects McCain had excelled in at the Naval Academy. He also reenacted famous American movies to entertain the troops, acting out scenes as best he remembered them. Other times, he improvised. "I did over a hundred movies," McCain told Timberg, "some of which I'd never seen."

Smoke rises from Haiphong, North Vietnam, during an American bombing raid, May 17, 1972. President Nixon's decision to escalate U.S. bombing of the enemy cheered McCain and fellow POWs and ultimately helped convince the North Vietnamese to negotiate a peace accord with the United States.

6

BOMBS BURSTING IN AIR

IF COMMUNICATING WITH fellow POWs was difficult, keeping in touch with loved ones back in the States was practically impossible. Each year, the Vietnamese forwarded no more than one or two of the numerous letters McCain had written to his wife. Only after two years in captivity was he permitted to send home a letter monthly.

Carol wrote to him frequently during his captivity, but few of her letters ever made it to him. Care packages containing food, clothes, and articles like vitamins rarely got through either, and prison officials and guards had usually ransacked the items that were delivered.

Such slights were minor compared with the physical and emotional abuse POWs endured during the late 1960s. Nearly all the men who were set free thereafter came home scarred physically or mentally. Untreated broken bones were commonplace. And for years, countless veterans would be plagued by a mental condition called post-traumatic stress disorder, a condition characterized by depression, anxiety attacks, flashbacks, and recurring nightmares.

Then, in September 1969, the North Vietnamese slowly but perceptibly began easing up on POWs. McCain said the change occurred shortly after the death of Ho Chi Minh, North Vietnam's leader. Throughout the 1960s Ho had condemned captured American servicemen as war criminals, all but ensuring that his followers would treat them cruelly. However, as American POWs were periodically released, stories of their inhumane treatment began trickling out, stirring up animosity against the North Vietnamese.

Fearing international reprisals, the Vietnamese stopped routinely beating prisoners and starving them into confessing. And on the Plantation, the most sadistic guards and commanders were either transferred to parts unknown or demoted. Suddenly, the North Vietnamese were anxious to show the world how well they were treating POWs.

John McCain's Christmas present in 1969 was being transferred from the Plantation back to Hoa Lo Prison, where his cellblock in the "Little Vegas" section of the compound was nicknamed "the Golden Nugget." By early spring, he was allowed to live with a roommate, ending two years of solitary confinement.

Although physical abuse was no longer routine, his obsession to communicate with fellow POWs—still a punishable offense—often landed him back in solitary lockup. "I had become very accustomed to close contact with my fellow prisoners since I had been released from solitary confinement," he said. "My state of mind had become so dependent on communicating with them that I worried my spell in isolation would fill me with such despair that I might break again. Blessedly, my fears were unfounded."

In late 1970, treatment had improved to the point that even habitual rule breakers like McCain were permitted outside their cells for several hours daily. "Prison life was improving, and it was about to get a whole lot better," he recalled.

One Christmas after he returned to the Hanoi Hilton, he was transferred yet another time to Camp Unity, a

McCain spent much of his time as a captive at the Hanoi Hilton, a former French colonial jail.

more communal jail where American prisoner ranks would eventually swell to 350. Among them were cherished friends like Bud Day. Best of all, however, was the simple pleasure of finally talking face-to-face with fellow POWs without fear of reprisal. "If you have never been deprived of liberty in solitude," said McCain, "you cannot know what ineffable joy you experience in the open company of other human beings, free to talk and joke without fear. The strength you acquire in fraternity with others who share your fate is immeasurable."

McCain and his joyful buddies talked away the first night together, about home, captivity, and the latest upturn in their fortunes. They were naturally suspicious about how long the even-handed treatment would last, but mostly they just rejoiced in one another's company.

The inmates used their newfound camaraderie to make a show of strength. Their rebellion was over religion. On February 7, 1971, Camp Unity prisoners decided to defy a prison rule forbidding groups of more than six from gathering or one man from speaking to a crowd. The edict effectively prevented men from gathering for church services.

American officers urged prisoners to conduct a service anyway, and dared camp officials to stop them by informing them that church was going to be held. Even after a North Vietnamese officer ordered the men to disperse, the worshipers, led by a four-man choir, continued. When guards hauled several ringleaders away, their American compatriots switched from solemn hymns to a rousing rendition of "The Star-Spangled Banner." Singing echoed through the prison, followed by rounds of applause.

It took a squad of soldiers in riot gear to still their voices. McCain and several others were led away at gunpoint for interrogation, which by now amounted to little more than animated scolding.

Prisoners were growing bolder in other areas as well. When the North Vietnamese, after years of blocking mail, began encouraging them to write letters home, the men decided that instead of cooperating with the propaganda ploy, they would refrain from writing until camp conditions—including lousy food—were upgraded.

The North Vietnamese, determined to regain the upper

hand over the Americans, responded to the civil disobedience by transferring the main troublemakers, including McCain, to a nearby prison called "Skid Row." The move was intended to punish the group by exposing them to harsher living conditions, among them solitary confinement in cramped cells with no lights, ventilation, or showers. "We had been singled out for our bad attitude, which I somewhat regretted, for it had cost me the open society of Camp Unity," recalled McCain. Yet he and his cohorts took some consolation in the knowledge that their uprising had earned a measure of fame back at Camp Unity, where they were now referred to as "the Hell's Angels."

After spending several months at Skid Row and in another, even more dismal, jail, McCain and his fellow POWs were returned to Camp Unity. He was overjoyed to once again be able to speak freely and circulate among his fellow prisoners. For the remainder of his incarceration there, most Americans were treated about as well as prisoners in an enemy country can be. They passed the monotonous days playing cards, performing bawdy skits, and boning up on academics—everything from quantum physics to English literature.

The biggest fear for POWs at this point was that they had been forgotten at home while the war lingered without resolution. "War is too horrible a thing to drag out unnecessarily," McCain would later write. Imagine his delight in April 1972 when President Richard Nixon decided to bomb the North Vietnamese into submission by ordering attacks on Hanoi and other targets for the first time in four years.

"Every POW knew that the harder the war was fought the sooner we would go home," McCain said. "Long aware of the on-and-off peace negotiations in Paris, we were elated when the Nixon administration proved it was intent on forcing the negotiations to a conclusion that would restore our freedom."

The ordeals of American POWs took an enormous toll on their loved ones at home. This page: The McCain family praying for the safe return of their husband and father at Thanksgiving. Opposite page: A hopeful letter from the POW.

Nixon unleashed a fierce bombing campaign. The ground beneath Hanoi shook from bombs exploding throughout the capital city, including some that blasted shrapnel into the heart of Camp Unity. And yet John McCain claims the bombs bursting in air were a dazzling fireworks show for captive POWs, who firmly believed their Independence Day was not far off.

The guards, on the other hand, ran for cover. "Many of them cowered in the shadows of our cellblocks," McCain recalled gleefully, "believing, correctly, that the B-52 pilots knew where Americans were held in Hanoi and were trying to avoid dropping their bombs on us."

For the first time, prison officials and guards began looking at their beleaguered captives in a new, almost respectful, light. Hanoi was feeling the full brunt of America's military might, and it didn't take a rocket scientist to realize who had the upper hand now.

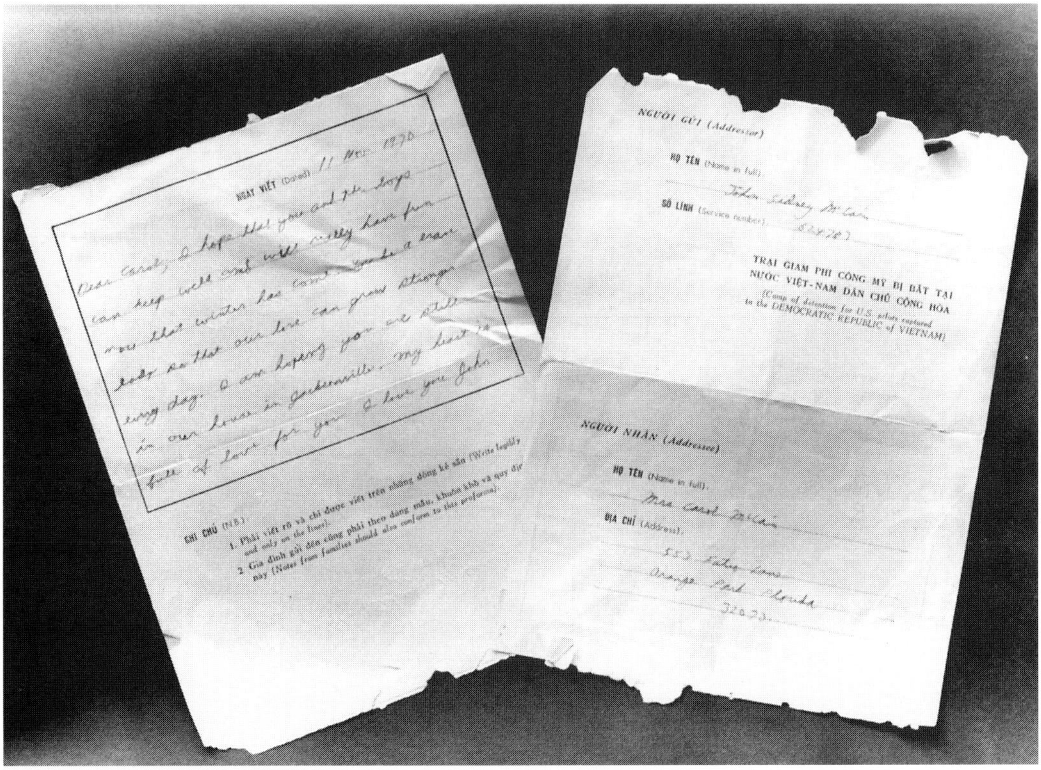

For 11 days U.S. B-52s rained bombs down on Hanoi and other Vietnamese strongholds. America's humbled foe got the message. On December 30, 1972, the bombing operation ceased. Nine days later, North Vietnamese and U.S. negotiators resumed peace talks in Paris. And on January 23, 1973, President Nixon told a grateful nation that an agreement ending the war had been hammered out. (Ultimately the Paris Agreement spelled the end only of American involvement in the war, and the North Vietnamese finally prevailed in April 1975.)

POWs didn't hear the blessed news of the Paris Agreement until five days afterward, when their captors assembled them in Camp Unity's courtyard. Even then they refrained from celebrating until back in the privacy of their cells. A North Vietnamese film crew on hand to

Free at last: McCain (at the front right) and his fellow POWs await transportation to Gia Lam Airport on the day of their release, March 15, 1973. Combative to the end, McCain tossed aside a new pair of crutches provided by the North Vietnamese, desiring, in his words, "to take my leave of Vietnam without any assistance from my hosts."

record their joyous reaction for posterity went home without the propaganda footage it was expecting.

The first POWs were scheduled for release two months later. Just as the Code of Conduct had decreed, they would return home in the order in which they'd been captured. Camp food was suddenly abundant and edible, and the days of beatings, torture, and solitary confinement were history.

On March 14, the day before John McCain was scheduled for release, the North Vietnamese commandant arranged a meeting during which he asked the navy flier if he wished to thank the doctor who had operated on his mangled knee years earlier. Spying a tape recorder in the room, McCain colorfully declined, saying that since he hadn't "seen the a——— in five years," he didn't see the point.

The next day, dressed in civilian garb, he and a contingent of fellow POWs stood at attention in front of a huge U.S. transport plane outside Hanoi. Their destination: Clark Air Force Base in the Philippines. The North Vietnamese had given McCain a brand-new pair of crutches for the occasion. But, determined to make a final defiant gesture, he tossed them aside and climbed aboard. "I wanted to take my leave of Vietnam without any assistance from my hosts," he said.

Once airborne and safely over the South China Sea, the assorted navy, marine, and air force pilots realized they were finally free men, and they acted accordingly, downing a picnic lunch with as much enthusiasm as if they were already home in their backyards in the States.

For John McCain, the moment was bittersweet. He and his comrades were indeed free. But these courageous survivors who had been beaten, starved, and imprisoned together were soon to go their separate ways. They would leave behind a dreadful period in their lives out of which human bonds had been formed that would endure a lifetime. "We were brothers now, as surely as if we had been born to the same parents," McCain said.

McCain, still hobbled by the injuries he sustained more than five years earlier, is welcomed home by President Richard M. Nixon.

7

THERE'S NO PLACE LIKE HOME

THE HOMEWARD-BOUND POWs were shocked at the throngs of well-wishers who greeted them at Clark Air Force Base and subsequent stops. After years of hearing from the North Vietnamese how disenchanted their fellow Americans had become with the war, a heroes' reception was the last thing they expected. "We were stunned and relieved to discover that most Americans were as happy to see us as we were to see them," recalled John McCain. "A lot of us were overcome by our reception, and the affection we were shown helped us to begin putting the war behind us."

Of course, many Americans *had* grown disenchanted with the war. Not all Vietnam veterans were greeted with parades, White House visits, or warm welcomes. Many servicemen would struggle for decades to gain a measure of respect and gratitude from a nation that had not always supported them in war or the painful years afterward.

John McCain knows that his years as a POW have opened some

doors for him, particularly in the political realm. He's been introduced countless times at public events as a hero who survived the worst the Vietnam War could dish out. Yet he recognizes that something in our national consciousness changed after Vietnam, a wound that took years to heal. "Surely, for a time, our loss in Vietnam afflicted America with a kind of identity crisis," he said in his memoirs. "For a while we made our way in the world less sure of ourselves than we had been before Vietnam. That was a pity, and I am relieved today that America's period of self-doubt has ended. . . . We were a good country before Vietnam, and we are a good country after Vietnam."

The America he and his fellow POWs remembered from 1967 was radically different in 1973. Lyndon Johnson had grown weary of the Vietnam War in 1968, declining to run for reelection and opening the door for Richard Nixon, a Republican, to ascend to the presidency. Nixon had arranged a peaceful end to the conflict, but not as soon as he'd promised. Moreover, he had made headlines for his role in another national crisis: Watergate, the scandal that would bring him down.

Senator Robert F. Kennedy and civil rights leader Martin Luther King Jr. had become martyrs of the '60s, assassinated in the prime of their lives. America had landed men on the moon, a goal first envisioned by President John F. Kennedy a decade earlier. On the entertainment front, the Beatles were history, although long hair was still in vogue among young men.

This was the landscape facing a man who had spent the last five and a half years in a prison camp. His challenge now? What to do for an encore.

For starters, McCain, now 36, had to renew acquaintances with his wife, Carol, who had been single-handedly raising their two sons and daughter in his absence. Being a single mom had been the lesser of Carol's tribulations. Several years before John's release, she had barely survived an auto accident that left her five inches shorter and dependent on crutches or a wheelchair. She managed to keep her secret from John until he stepped off the C-141 in the Philippines and was informed by navy officials.

When he called Carol at home in Florida, she prepared him for the worst. "John," she said, "it was really bad. You might be upset when you see me."

"Well, you know, I don't look so good myself," he cracked. "It's fine."

They celebrated their reunion by buying a modest beach house in Florida. Meanwhile, John thought long and hard about his future. He was eager to climb back into a navy jet, but his injuries made doing so extremely difficult. Just raising his arms above his head was impossible. His injured right knee was in even worse shape, allowing him little mobility.

He spent three months in a military hospital, where doctors initially hoped to rehabilitate his worst injuries. Too much time had elapsed since they'd been inflicted, however, and the physicians had little success. The doctors implied that McCain's flying days were over.

His years of confinement had only made him more determined than ever to overcome adversity. When the navy said it could do nothing more, McCain hired a private physical therapist who literally put her shoulder against his knee day after day until it eventually began bending again. A few painful months later, he insisted he was physically able to fly, a fact that navy doctors seemed helpless to overrule. Whether it was safe for him to fly was another question. McCain himself wondered whether he could reach up high enough to pull the ejector lever if he ever had to bail out.

While undergoing physical therapy, McCain spent his days attending the National War College on the outskirts of Washington, D.C. He devoured books about Vietnam, apparently eager to learn what forces had led

Carol, Doug, Andy, John, and Sydney McCain at their home in Jacksonville, Florida. Though life seemed idyllic after John's release, the McCains' marriage would soon disintegrate.

the United States to wage a losing war it now seemed anxious to forget. Following a year of study, he concluded, "Those who were better off economically did not carry out their obligations, so we forced the Hispanic, the ghetto black, and the Appalachian white to fight and die. That to me was the great crime and injustice of the Vietnam War."

Then he vowed to move beyond Vietnam, as if it were an assigned chapter in his life he could retire to a scrapbook in his mind, where it would gather dust along with other unpleasant periods, like his first year at the Naval Academy. When people asked for details about his years as a POW, he usually resisted. "I don't talk about prison because it bores the s——— out of me," he once stated.

As a testament to his tenacity, John McCain did fly again, commanding a Replacement Air Group back in Jacksonville, Florida. It was a plum assignment that culminated when the group received its first-ever commendation.

While his flying career was ending on a high note, McCain's marriage to Carol was withering on the vine. For a time after his return they had been inseparable. Giddy as teenagers experiencing first love, they'd hobble into homecoming celebrations on crutches, so happy to be alive they'd forget how close they'd both come to dying.

But the two had lived worlds apart for more than five years. During that forced separation each had endured personal tragedy without the other's support.

Carol didn't necessarily see it that way, however, musing that their marriage may not have endured even if John had never been to Vietnam. She told Timberg, "I attribute it more to John turning forty and wanting to be twenty-five again than I do to anything else."

The McCains' on-again, off-again marriage survived until 1980. Meanwhile, in 1977, his career was in limbo. Although he had finagled his way back into flying, even he knew his days in a cockpit were numbered. For a bona fide Vietnam celebrity, John McCain had surprisingly few prospects awaiting him once he planted his feet back on the ground permanently.

He nearly settled on a staff assignment that would have led to obscurity, but the brass had other ideas and transferred him to the U.S. Navy's Senate liaison office in Washington, D.C., a post once held by his father. Liaisons served as conduits of information between the navy and Congress—or, more accurately perhaps, represented the navy's interests before members of Congress. In a sense, they were lobbyists. Never one to become starry-eyed in the presence of the famous or powerful, McCain would use his position to effectively court Capitol Hill's movers and shakers.

John McCain had always enjoyed being the center of attention. He had inspired bored midshipmen to join him on unauthorized drinking binges at Annapolis. He had turned Meridian, Mississippi, into a favored watering hole for navy sky jockeys. And he had been dragged kicking and screaming to solitary confinement while his fellow POWs cheered from their cells. When he walked into a room now, people paid attention to John McCain—even on Capitol Hill.

He shot the breeze with "plebe" senators as well as those upperclassmen who held the nation's reins—men like John Tower, the most powerful Republican on the Armed Services Committee. "John McCain, as a Navy captain, knew on a personal basis more senators and was more warmly received than virtually any lobbyist I have ever known in this town; they loved to see him," Jim McGovern, a junior officer who served on his staff, told Timberg.

And McCain, emboldened by his view of failed Vietnam policy, didn't shy away from using his Senate contacts to accomplish navy aims—even if the president saw things differently. In one instance illustrated in *The Nightingale's Song,* the navy sorely wanted Congress to authorize billions for a nuclear-powered aircraft carrier. President Jimmy Carter, a Democrat, vetoed an entire defense-spending bill just to kill the carrier's funding. But working quietly behind closed doors in the Senate, John McCain made it his mission to resurrect the carrier funding. A

The war hero, now a U.S. Navy liaison, with some of the Senate's movers and shakers. From left: John Glenn, McCain, William Cohen, Barry Goldwater. McCain would eventually fill Goldwater's U.S. Senate seat.

year later, it was again authorized by Congress and signed by a reluctant Carter.

Successes like these aside, McCain was restless, both in his professional and personal life. He couldn't imagine being a navy liaison indefinitely, any more than he could picture himself commanding an aircraft carrier. His career in the navy had peaked, and his marriage was on the rocks. He decided it was time for a change. In early 1980, he and Carol divorced. Three months later, he

John McCain was 43 when he married 26-year-old Cindy Hensley in 1980.

married Cindy Hensley, a refined, blonde-haired beauty from Arizona whose father had made a fortune distributing beer. John was 43, Cindy 26.

On the career front, McCain, now a navy captain, recognized that becoming a four-star admiral like his father and grandfather wasn't in the cards. Yet how he played his next hand could determine whether he lived up to their achievements. Perhaps the answer lay in politics. Even his own father had courted Washington power brokers throughout much of his career, recognizing that this was how dreams became reality in the nation's capital. All John McCain had to figure out now was how and where to get elected.

Vice President Dan Quayle swears in the Republican senator from Arizona as the proud McCain family looks on.

8

MR. McCAIN GOES TO WASHINGTON

McCAIN RETIRED FROM the navy and turned his sights to Cindy's home state of Arizona. She had grown up in Phoenix, a city that had experienced rapid growth like many other developing areas of the Southwest. There was so much population growth in Phoenix that, based on the 1980 census, Arizona was gaining another seat in the U.S. House of Representatives. The timing couldn't be better, McCain figured. The fact that it was already 1981, less than a year before elections would be held, didn't faze him. Neither did the fact he wasn't an Arizona resident—nor had he ever been, for that matter.

He began his apprenticeship in politics by enlisting a seasoned political consultant whose first piece of advice was don't barge into town and tell everyone you moved to Arizona to get elected to Congress. After moving to Phoenix, McCain volunteered for the Arizona Republican Party and began raising money for it statewide. Naturally, he also introduced himself to anyone who would return his handshake.

He was a natural politician. There were just two problems: he couldn't reveal his scheme to run for election; and even if he could, there was still no place to run. The House seat he expected to open up in Phoenix had instead been allocated to Tucson.

Just when the outlook was gloomiest, a glimmer of light broke through. John Rhodes, a Republican representing Phoenix's First Congressional District, announced he was retiring. The former POW turned politician-in-waiting suddenly had an open seat to shoot for. Of course, at the time he didn't even live in the First Congressional District. No matter. Before the day ended, he and Cindy had bought a new house there.

Heeding his consultant's advice, John McCain cooled his heels until early spring, when he officially jumped into the Republican primary race. Of the four candidates, he was considered the least likely to win.

But this time as new kid on the block, McCain was a man with a mission. He knocked on doors of Republican voters around Phoenix like a vacuum cleaner salesman peddling his wares. Before long, homeowners stopped asking him what he was selling and started paying attention to his election pitch. The catchy TV commercials he could now pay for thanks to several hundred thousand dollars in campaign funds he'd raised, some courtesy of his father-in-law's beer fortune, helped as well.

The biggest obstacle he faced was skepticism. People were naturally suspicious of a candidate who had lived in his adopted state for only one year. He didn't come up with a good answer to the "outsider" question until asked about it for the hundredth time while he was at a candidate forum. His legendary temper boiled over like a radiator in Arizona's sweltering summer heat.

"Listen, pal," he began when asked whether he needed Arizona more than it needed him. "I spent twenty-two years in the Navy. My father was in the Navy. My grandfather was in the Navy. We in the military service tend to move a lot. We have to live in all parts of the country, all parts of the world. I wish I could have had the luxury, like you, of growing up and living and spending my entire life in a nice place like the First District of Arizona, but I was doing other things.

"As a matter of fact," he added, "when I think about it now, the place I lived longest in my life was Hanoi."

It was a classic, off-the-cuff McCainism, and it silenced his critics. He went on to win the 1982 Republican primary, and in the general election he trounced his Democratic opponent.

Two years later, he astonished his doubters a second time by winning reelection by an even larger margin. True, he had come to Washington a known commodity, a war hero with connections. But he also remembered who had elected him to office in the first place. During his first year in the House, he flew home nearly every weekend to meet with Phoenix-area voters, speak at public gatherings, and spend time with Cindy, who had decided to live there as a full-time mother. The McCains' new family would grow to include Meghan, Jack, Jimmy, and an adopted daughter, Bridget.

Like many politicians, however, John McCain couldn't help musing about the future. In 1984, Arizona's Barry Goldwater, perhaps America's most conservative national politician at the time, was on the verge of retiring. McCain badly wanted his U.S. Senate seat. In fact, he may have coveted it from the day he first set foot in Arizona. One likely opponent was Arizona governor Bruce Babbitt, a Democrat said to be interested in running for president someday.

But Babbitt decided not to challenge McCain and never entered the race. His decision allowed John McCain to breeze to a Senate election victory in 1986, only five years after moving to Arizona. Political commentators were already gushing over the white-haired wonder as an up-and-coming star on the national scene. There was even mention of him as a possible running mate for George H. W. Bush, Ronald Reagan's vice president at the time and the likely Republican nominee for the presidency in 1988.

Bush ended up tapping another vice presidential candidate. He settled on Dan Quayle, a relatively unknown U.S. senator whose rise to prominence would be diminished by a tendency to stick his foot in his mouth. Meanwhile, John McCain was padding his résumé in the Senate, serving on the Commerce Committee and the Science and Transportation Committee. And despite his tortured past in Vietnam, he urged his colleagues and the nation to reconcile with their former enemy. McCain himself had visited Vietnam several times since 1973.

Although McCain was enjoying smooth sailing, stormy weather loomed on the horizon. In 1989, a news story first published in Arizona began making waves in Washington. According to the press reports, McCain and four other influential senators had tried to help Charles Keating fend off federal scrutiny of Lincoln Savings and Loan Association, a California thrift institution he owned. Journalists implied that the politicians were beholden to Keating because he had lined their campaign coffers with thousands of dollars in contributions over the years. McCain himself had accepted more than $100,000 from Keating or his associates.

When Lincoln ultimately went bankrupt, like scores of other savings and loans across the country, many depositors lost every cent they had entrusted to the institution. Subsequently, the federal government—through American taxpayers—was forced to spend billions repairing the financial meltdown.

After lengthy Senate Ethics Committee hearings on the matter, McCain was cleared of serious wrongdoing and blamed for "poor judgment" more than anything.

John McCain visits Hanoi under happier circumstances, 1985. The former POW consistently advocated reconciliation with Vietnam.

Nevertheless, the sordid affair tested his resolve and temporarily soured his aspirations for higher office. He had seriously considered retiring from politics altogether at the peak of public indignation, and it would take years for people to stop referring to him as one of the "Keating Five." According to Robert Timberg, McCain told disbelieving Senate staffers during the ordeal, "This is the worst thing, the absolute worst thing that ever happened to me."

But instead of riding off into the Arizona sunset when the furor died down, he summoned a burst of energy from his depleted reserves and barnstormed across the state in his 1992 reelection bid. The odds were against him when the race began thanks to the unfavorable press coverage. But on Election Day, he again prevailed by a wide margin.

McCain's second six-year term in the Senate saw him regain much of the political luster that had been dulled by the Keating scandal. His colleagues and the country paid attention each time the former POW expressed reservations about thrusting U.S. troops into the globe's latest hot spot, whether it was Panama or Somalia. A speech he gave during a commencement address to Marine Corps officers shed light on his reluctance to put American troops in harm's way. "I have memories of a place so far removed from the comforts of this blessed country that I have learned to forget some of the anguish it once brought me," McCain said. "But my happiness these last twenty years has not let me forget the friends who did not return with me to the country we loved so dearly. The memory of them, of what they bore for honor and country, causes me to look in every prospective conflict for the shadow of Vietnam."

After the Keating affair, McCain also launched a crusade to reform campaign finance laws to avoid the possibility—or even the appearance—that big donors might receive favors from politicians in return for their financial backing. His task was herculean. Since there have been politicians, there have been people offering them money with the expectation of getting something in return. Charles Keating was just the latest, most notorious, example.

Today, individuals and businesses can donate no more than $1,000 annually to a politician's campaign. But there's no limit whatsoever on how much they can con-

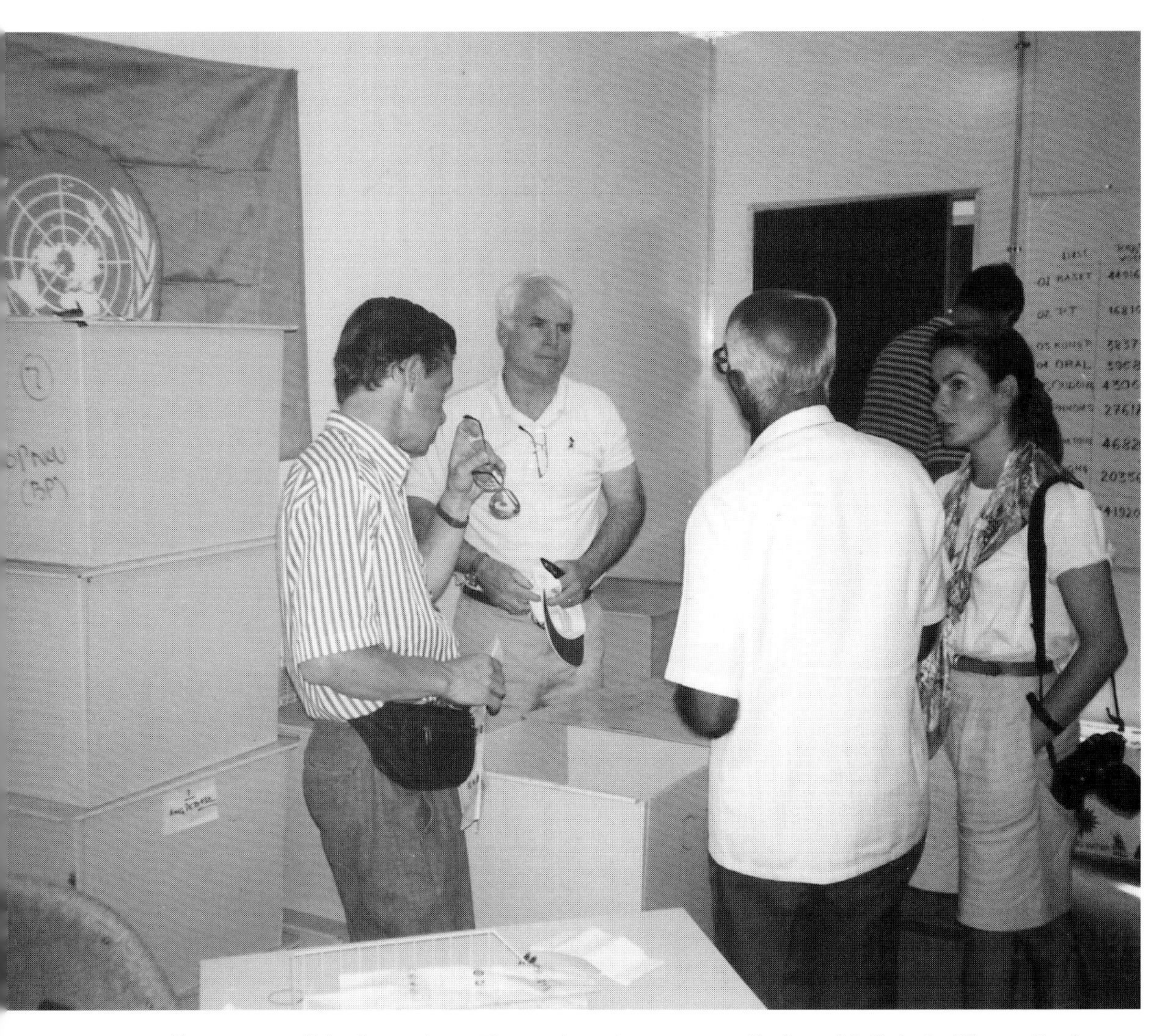

McCain in Phnom Penh, Cambodia, as part of a team of election observers, May 1983. While calling for a strong national defense and active involvement in world affairs, McCain has expressed concern about putting American troops in harm's way in ill-defined missions.

tribute to political parties. These donations are called "soft money," and McCain has tried for a decade to ban them. Doing so has earned him the scorn of powerful members of his own party as well as those Democrats who see soft money as the lifeblood of the political system. To say his battle was uphill would be an understatement. At least it was a familiar position.

Because he faced stiff opposition from fellow Republicans, McCain courted sympathetic Democrats in his quest to change campaign finance laws. "Reaching across the aisle" was a familiar strategy for McCain. When he was elected to the House, he struck up a lasting friendship with fellow Arizona lawmaker Mo Udall, as liberal a Democrat as there was at the time. Nonetheless, it was Udall he publicly thanked four years later—rather than Barry Goldwater—after he won his Senate race.

McCain also joined forces with Democratic senator John Kerry of Massachusetts, a Vietnam veteran who shared his resolve to determine the fate of American servicemen missing in action (MIA). As part of their investigation, the pair visited North Vietnam, where they were given access to thousands of photographs taken of U.S. personnel during the war. Among the other artifacts they brought home was the flight helmet John McCain had been wearing when he was shot down over Hanoi.

Their teamwork resulted in the American government's decision to release previously classified documentation on MIAs. Ultimately, Kerry and McCain's bipartisan committee concluded that it was unlikely any U.S. servicemen remained captive in Vietnam.

McCain's closest ally in the Senate during the 1990s was probably Democrat Russell Feingold of Wisconsin. Their distaste for campaign funding practices drew them together. In 1995, they sponsored the McCain-Feingold reform bill, aimed at eliminating soft money contributions. After the bill died—neither party really wanted it—McCain and Feingold vowed to reintroduce the legislation every year until meaningful campaign reform was enacted.

McCain and Feingold also attacked "pork-barrel" spending, the money quietly approved each year for pet projects in individual congressional districts or states. Several members of the House and Senate were notorious for "bringing home the bacon." McCain was never shy about denouncing the practice, regardless of whom he offended. He once recommended slashing in half the $198 million allocated for a federal courthouse planned for Phoenix, exasperating his fellow senator from Arizona, who had spearheaded the legislation.

With Cindy at a 1999 campaign rally in South Carolina shortly after announcing his entry into the 2000 presidential race. McCain's straight-talking style, combined with his compelling personal story, caught the attention of the media as well as disillusioned voters around the country.

9

THE STRAIGHT TALK EXPRESS

BY THE TIME Bill Clinton's presidency began winding down in the late 1990s, he had something in common with John McCain: his political enemies vastly outnumbered his allies. Although Clinton had governed the nation during some of the most prosperous years in American history, Republicans attributed his success to fortunate timing rather than savvy stewardship. Moreover, they felt that he had desecrated the Oval Office by having an affair with a White House intern and then doing everything in his power to survive the scandal.

But the two-term president would have to step aside after the 2000 election, and as the presidential primary season approached, Republican Party leaders began searching for a candidate who could recapture the White House from the Democrats.

George W. Bush, governor of Texas, seemed to fit that bill. Bush could look presidential, had a relatively successful record in Texas, and was the son of a former president with powerful connections among the party's deep-pocketed patrons. All these attributes translated into a bankable candidate. Long before he officially announced his intentions to seek the Republican nomination for president, Bush's campaign war chest overflowed with millions of dollars, and his endorsements read like a Who's Who of Republican heavyweights.

Almost overnight he attained the stature of a Goliath. All the more reason, naturally, for John McCain to play David and run for president himself. If anyone was comfortable flinging stones at giants, it was he.

McCain announced his candidacy on April 14, 1999, nearly a year before the first primary contest. His assets included a familiar name, a touring bus called the Straight Talk Express, and his legendary zeal for undertaking crusades others considered long shots. His liabilities consisted of meager campaign finances by George W. Bush standards and a glaring absence of meaningful political endorsements. Of 55 Republican senators, only 4 backed him. If he were going to win the Republican nomination, it would have to be without the benefit of traditional party resources.

As in the Senate, McCain appealed to people outside his mainstream, notably Independents and Democrats, who were permitted in several state primaries to vote for candidates in different parties. And instead of spending his limited funds on TV ads promoting his campaign, he welcomed media coverage with open arms—a strategy that endeared him to the national press and guaranteed free publicity as long as his candidacy still had a pulse.

Spring primary races determine the major parties' presidential candidates in the fall general election. In most states, the winner of the primary earns a certain number of delegates who then typically vote for the victor at each party's national convention the following summer. Whoever gained the majority of delegates first in 2000—in the Republicans' case, 1,034—essentially locked up the party nomination.

Short on funds but long on energy, McCain launched a

ground campaign that would have won him commendations in combat. He had never been shy about "pressing flesh" on the campaign trail, and he set off in the Straight Talk Express to visit states where he could meet likely voters face-to-face.

The first test of a presidential candidacy is Iowa, which doesn't hold a primary election per se but rather what is called a straw poll at the party's state caucuses. Because only those voters who travel to the caucuses can vote, the Iowa straw poll favors candidates who have solid political organizations and abundant money—candidates like George W. Bush and millionaire publisher Steve Forbes. McCain campaign strategists considered the Hawkeye State a lost cause and bypassed it for New Hampshire, which holds the first primary election.

Independent-minded voters in New Hampshire often favor mavericks, and in 2000 McCain felt right at home. His campaign preached familiar Republican themes like lower taxes and strengthening the military. However, it was his platform on campaign finance reform that resonated with Granite State voters.

McCain's war record didn't hurt either. On the campaign trail, McCain downplayed it, saying, "It doesn't take a lot of talent to intercept a surface-to-air missile with your airplane." Yet, whether he intended it to or not, his Vietnam ordeal inspired admiration. Enthusiastic crowds flocked to hear his reformer's message in town halls across the state. Many voters clutching *Faith of My Fathers* rushed up to shake their hero's hand or get an autograph.

George W. Bush was receiving a chillier response in icy New Hampshire. Partly that was because he distanced himself from voters and the press, preferring to deliver carefully scripted speeches and "sound bites" guaranteed to keep him out of hot water. He could afford that luxury; he was the front-runner, not a candidate running for his political life. But the governor of Texas would soon find

Campaign scene, Manchester, New Hampshire, January 16, 2000. Known for their support of independent-minded politicians, New Hampshire voters would hand McCain a stunning primary victory—and rock the Republican establishment.

out that even the odds-on favorite can stumble if he believes victory is all but inevitable. And the challenge came not from Steve Forbes, but from a former midshipman nearly expelled from Annapolis.

New Hampshire voters turned out en masse in the closely watched February 2000 primary and handed John McCain a stunning win. He beat Bush, the favored Republican son, by 19 percent. The coronation that previously seemed certain had been, at the very least, postponed indefinitely. "A wonderful New Hampshire campaign has come to an end, but a great national crusade has just begun," McCain yelled in a victory celebration.

The Straight Talk Express was on a roll. The campaign's heavily promoted Internet website, which accepted online contributions, was overloaded by donors. Before sunrise the day after the New Hampshire primary, $300,000 had flowed in from credit card contributions. A week later, the tally had mushroomed to $2 million and 22,000 volunteers had come onboard. During the entire campaign, *mccain2000.com* would raise an estimated $10 million.

A stunned Bush camp huddled in strategy sessions to analyze what went wrong in New Hampshire and decide how to prevent a recurrence. The next big contest was in South Carolina, a stronghold of Christian conservatives. Bush operatives feverishly manned phone banks, praising his candidacy and condemning McCain's.

South Carolina was familiar territory for McCain. He had begun stumping there long before the New Hampshire primary. Few voters recognized him at the time as he shook hands wherever crowds gathered, including hometown baseball games. How times had changed. The week after his upset win in New Hampshire, South Carolinians treated him like a rock star. In his speeches, he didn't disappoint. "You have my solemn promise. I will always tell you the truth, no matter what," he vowed in a jab at the Clinton White House.

Ironically, truth was the first campaign casualty in South Carolina. Pamphlets began circulating saying that Cindy McCain had been a drug addict. Bush officials disavowed the mudslinging, but that did little to ease Cindy McCain's grief. She had indeed become addicted to painkillers in the early 1990s after a slow recovery from back surgery. She had even stolen pain medication from the children's relief organization she'd founded. When an investigation revealed the missing drugs, she'd been forced to confront the theft and her addiction. Following the disclosure, an Arizona newspaper had ridiculed her in a cartoon, infuriating John McCain.

Still, Cindy had put the embarrassing episode behind her, convinced she was a stronger person because of it. But now the pro-Bush campaign pamphlets reopened that old wound, once again angering her husband and, presumably, reflecting badly on his candidacy.

Other attacks bore even less resemblance to the truth. Bush publicly embraced a disgruntled Vietnam vet who alleged that McCain had forgotten fellow veterans after returning from the war. Instead of turning the other cheek, a livid McCain agreed to an ad comparing Bush with Clinton. The ad's narrator said, "Isn't it time we had a president who told the truth?"

In the end, the character attacks overwhelmed McCain's defenses. Bush won South Carolina and was back in the driver's seat. To the astonishment of many observers, the majority of voters polled after the election said Bush had run the cleaner campaign.

Campaign 2000 now swung to Michigan, a pivotal primary state whose Democrats and Independents could vote for Republicans in the primary. McCain pulled out all the stops, pleading with voters of all affiliations—including those in his own party who distrusted his reformist platform—to climb aboard the Straight Talk Express. "Don't fear this campaign, my fellow Republicans. Join it! Join it!" he beckoned.

Bush, meanwhile, eased up on the gas in Michigan, giving the distinct impression that he was looking past his Republican primary opponents to Vice President Al Gore, his presumed Democratic opponent in the fall general election. John Engler, the Republican governor of Michigan, had thrown his clout behind Bush, as had virtually every other Republican governor. Once again, however, George W. Bush underestimated the appeal of John McCain and his straight-talking message.

Turnout was nearly three times higher than usual, and Michigan voters handed McCain another upset victory. He swept his home state of Arizona as well. Bush, who suddenly seemed vulnerable, now had to devote more money and time toward winning the nomination his supporters had thought would be a foregone conclusion.

In the aftermath of the Michigan loss, Bush supporters

The McCains were smiling at this rally after the primary loss in South Carolina, but the tactics adopted by George W. Bush and his supporters rankled.

grumbled about the McCain campaign's tactics. McCain volunteers in Michigan had telephoned hundreds of voters to inform them that Bush had appeared at Bob Jones University, a conservative school in South Carolina with a reputation for anti-Catholic rhetoric. The inference McCain's volunteers wanted the voters to draw, Bush supporters said, was that the Texas governor himself was anti-Catholic. In response to these charges, McCain loyalists pointed to the attacks Bush supporters had earlier launched in South Carolina.

As the sniping continued, neither candidate appeared as virtuous as he had when primary season began. The battle shifted to Virginia, another conservative southern state where Bush had an organizational edge. His early advantage solidified when McCain figuratively shot himself in the foot at a rally in Virginia Beach by saying, "Neither party should be defined by pandering to the outer reaches of American politics and the agents of intolerance, whether they be Louis Farrakhan or Al Sharpton on the left, or Pat Robertson or Jerry Falwell on the right."

McCain blamed Falwell and Robertson, politically active Christian leaders fervently behind Bush, for spreading falsehoods about his campaign and character in recent weeks. He sealed his fate the following day by calling them "forces of evil." McCain's words alienated Christian conservatives, who form a sizable voting bloc in Virginia. By a 4-1 majority, they voted for Bush, guaranteeing the Texas governor an easy victory.

McCain campaign officials knew they were in trouble. On March 7, a day dubbed Super Tuesday, 16 states—including such delegate-rich battlegrounds as New York, Ohio, and the biggest prize of all, California—would be holding their primaries. Super Tuesday would make or break McCain's campaign: unless he won at least some of the states, his presidential hopes for the year 2000 were over.

Bush's superior organization and finances once again gave him the upper hand. Nevertheless, he was taking little for granted. His backers ran ads in New York saying McCain had voted against funding for breast cancer research. John McCain was so incensed about the spurious ads he couldn't even summon an answer for reporters seeking a response. His own sister, Sandy, had been stricken with cancer. "I hope my sister wasn't watching the news tonight" was all he managed. Another anonymous group's ads criticized McCain's environmental voting record.

The ads may have taken liberties with the truth, but in the days leading up to Super Tuesday they kept McCain on the defensive. While the Bush campaign ran on all cylinders, McCain's wheels were falling off. He spent most of his time fuming publicly about the attack ads, several of which were funded not by the Bush campaign itself, but by wealthy supporters whose identity was often difficult to uncover. It was a clever way to circumvent the kinds of campaign finance reforms that John McCain had been advocating for years.

Not all the news for the Arizona senator was grim. In Sacramento, California, a mother attending a town-hall meeting for McCain inadvertently presented him with a Kodak moment. Saying she had been embarrassed to explain President Clinton's scandalous behavior to her two young daughters, she asked, "Will you truly bring dignity and courage to the White House?" And by the way, she quickly added, "Can my son shake your hand?"

Even diehard liberal publications like the *New Republic* tried to boost McCain's chances. In its March 6 issue, it took the unprecedented step of endorsing his candidacy, saying that "for the first time in recent memory, a serious Republican presidential candidate is seeking to remake his party into something other than the political arm of the privileged few. . . . all Americans concerned about the integrity and decency of our political system should make his cause their own."

Not enough Americans, particularly Republicans, agreed. On March 7, voters in 12 of the 16 states holding primaries chose Bush's cause over McCain's. California and New York, two delegate-rich states, were among those that backed Bush.

It was the stroke of midnight for McCain's Cinderella presidential bid. Two days later, he officially concluded his fairytale candidacy in Arizona by "suspending" his campaign. "We knew when we began this campaign that ours was a difficult challenge," he said in a press conference. "Last Tuesday, that challenge became considerably more difficult as a majority of Republican voters made clear their preference for president is Governor Bush."

McCain conceded the nomination battle to Bush, but pointedly withheld his endorsement as well as the delegates he had earned in the primaries. Some followers urged him

His chances for victory having evaporated with the Super Tuesday balloting, McCain announces his withdrawal from the Republican presidential campaign, Sedona, Arizona, March 9, 2000.

to join the Reform Party or run as an Independent candidate in the general election. He dashed such speculation, saying the Republican Party was his "home."

Many Republicans feared that the primaries had divided their party. Bush had also spent much more money locking up the nomination than he'd wanted, leaving his reserves depleted for what promised to be a bruising presidential race with Al Gore. In addition, John McCain still held the high ground when it came to uniting his party. And whether his detractors liked it or not, he was in a strong position to dictate the terms of peace negotiations with the Bush forces.

When McCain returned to Capitol Hill on March 20, the senator who had always been an outsider was greeted with a standing ovation from his colleagues. More cynical observers speculated that the applause was recognition of his celebrity status rather than genuine affection. This much was certain, however: legislators who had never been in McCain's camp, especially those up for reelection, suddenly decided he wasn't such a bad fellow after all.

"Despite getting knocked out of the presidential race with eight months to go, McCain has emerged as the Michael Jordan of American politics, the most coveted endorsement around," observed *CQ Weekly*.

Dozens of House Republicans who were worried about losing their seats asked McCain to campaign on their behalf, knowing full well that his newfound luster could rub off on them. The Arizona senator responded by forming Straight Talk America, a political action committee through which he could solicit contributions on behalf of Republicans facing tough campaigns.

Of course, by agreeing to hit the campaign trail on behalf of candidates eager to capitalize on his popularity, McCain ensured that he would remain in the spotlight as well. After all, there was always 2004. "With the campaign over, we wanted to make sure that Sen. McCain continued to have a platform and a megaphone in order to continue to influence not only the Republican Party, but American politics as well," said a campaign aide.

By the time Americans went to the polls for the general election, John McCain had logged 53,643 air miles, 6,898 road miles, and 251 rail miles stumping for congressional candidates. No one can say with certainty whether his support made a difference to those Republicans, but it probably didn't hurt. More than half of them won their races, guaranteeing Republican control of the House through 2002.

As for supporting George W. Bush, that was a gesture Senator McCain seemed in no hurry to make after the bitter primary battle. The campaign wounds were too deep to heal overnight.

In war and politics, many adversaries have underestimated John McCain's determination and resilience. Though defeated in the 2000 presidential campaign, he soon got back into the political fray in the U.S. Senate. Among McCain's most burning goals is the enactment of legislation to reform the way American political campaigns are financed.

10

PATRON SAINT OF LOST CAUSES

IF GEORGE W. BUSH sincerely wanted John McCain's endorsement, he was courting it in a peculiar way. Less than one month after his Super Tuesday victories, Bush had grown so weary of hearing McCain's name he felt obliged to remind a *New York Times* reporter that it was he, not the Arizona senator, who had won the most primaries. His tone made people wonder whether he wanted to "bury the hatchet" in his former opponent's head.

However, Bush aides as well as McCain's handlers knew that both sides would have to negotiate a peace treaty, hopefully long before the Republican National Convention in August. Otherwise, Bush could hardly continue proclaiming himself "a uniter, not a divider." The trouble was, Bush strategists seemed uncertain just how strongly to woo McCain, whose celebrity status was earning him higher approval ratings than Al Gore, Bill Clinton, or George W. Bush.

Some political analysts said Bush owed McCain a debt of gratitude for whipping him into shape in the primaries. Bush the anointed son was forced to become George the brawler, the thinking went, thus preparing him for the showdown with Al Gore. "Prior to New Hampshire, Bush was sleepwalking," wrote columnist Don Feder in *Human Events.* "McCain's early victories shocked the governor out of his stupor and put him in the combat mode he'll need to win in November."

After playing hard to get for several months, McCain finally offered his hand to Bush, in Pittsburgh. On May 9, the victor and runner-up stood side by side, though looking somewhat uncomfortable, as John McCain officially backed the Republican nominee. He didn't use the "E" word, however, until a chorus of reporters pointed out the omission. "I endorse Governor Bush. I endorse Governor Bush. I endorse Governor Bush," McCain chanted . . . seven times.

Not to be outdone, Bush added, "By the way, I enthusiastically accept."

McCain's troops said he offered to campaign on Bush's behalf from then till Election Day in November. But it was clear that day in Pittsburgh the two had reached an uneasy truce at best. "So far," a McCain aide told *Human Events,* "we have not been asked" to campaign.

Rumors had been swirling that Bush might appease his vanquished foe by offering him a seat in his future White House cabinet, perhaps as secretary of defense. There was also talk of naming him as his vice presidential pick, a move that could ensure crucial votes from the Independents and crossover Democrats who had backed McCain.

McCain shot down any notion of signing on as vice president when Bush broached the topic in Pittsburgh. Aside from his personal and philosophical differences with Bush and his reluctance to be relegated to the largely ceremonial post of vice president, McCain had another reason for removing himself from consideration. In 1996 he'd been asked by Republican nominee Bob Dole to consider being his vice president, which required an intensive review of his and Cindy's finances, a fiscal

Looking more than a bit uncomfortable, McCain officially endorses George W. Bush at the Westin Hotel in Pittsburgh, May 9, 2000.

strip search they weren't anxious to relive.

The media spent the next few months speculating whom Bush might select as a running mate. Names like Senator Fred Thompson of Tennessee, Governor Frank Keating of Oklahoma, and Representative Chris Cox of California appeared in print. So did John McCain's, despite his persistent denials that he was interested. In the end, Bush surprised nearly everyone by settling on Dick Cheney, a former congressman and secretary of defense during Bush's father's presidency. Ironically, Cheney had been picked to head the vice president search team for Governor Bush's campaign.

In late July, tensions were running high on the eve of the Republican National Convention in Philadelphia. Party leaders were determined to show a more unified front than they had in 1996, when issues like abortion threatened to split the Republican Party into warring factions.

They needn't have worried. Despite rolling into town aboard the Straight Talk Express with TV crews in tow, John McCain didn't steal the show. Nor did the 160 out of 2,066 delegates he had won in the primaries embarrass everyone else by proposing that McCain be the nominee on the convention floor.

His address before the packed convention was neither divisive nor half-hearted. "I'm proud to join you this evening in commending to all Americans the man who now represents your best wishes and mine for the future of our country, my friend, Governor George W. Bush, the next president of the United States," he said.

Following the convention, McCain was back on the campaign trail on behalf of congressional Republicans. But two weeks later, his ability to withstand a punch was tested yet again. In an August 18 press conference, McCain revealed that he was undergoing surgery to have two cancerous lesions removed: one on his left temple and another on his left arm. Biopsies indicated melanoma, the fastest-spreading, deadliest form of skin cancer. Six years earlier, he had undergone surgery to have a similar melanoma removed from his shoulder.

"I've been in a number of fights in my life, and this is just another one, and I'm sure we will be able to prevail," said the 63-year-old senator. McCain and his doctors at Phoenix's Mayo Clinic hoped the aggressive cancer had not spread, and subsequent surgery appeared to confirm their hopes. Not long after Labor Day, McCain returned to Washington after being declared cancer-free.

He promptly set off again stumping for fellow Republicans, whether or not they agreed with him on what had become his most prominent issue, campaign finance reform. What most people couldn't help noticing, however, was how few times he rallied the troops for George W. Bush.

McCain's advisers said the senator had offered to work double-time on the Republican nominee's behalf, but so far he hadn't gotten the call from the bullpen very often.

Though himself out of the running for president, McCain used his newfound popularity to campaign for Republicans around the country, including Indiana gubernatorial hopeful David McIntosh (shown here).

Political insiders speculated that the Bush team was keeping its distance from McCain, fearful he would say or do something on the spur of the moment that could hurt Bush's chances.

There were the usual whisper campaigns saying John McCain didn't want to commit wholeheartedly to Bush's race on the off-chance the governor might lose to Al Gore—and thus give McCain another shot at the presidency in 2004. *Newsweek* noted that the Arizona senator was "visibly pained" by the suggestion that he "sold out his supporters by endorsing Bush after their ugly fight."

"Probably nothing on this earth bothers him more," a McCain aide told the magazine.

The two former rivals did share the stage in New

England the week before Election Day. But even that joint appearance didn't go off without a hitch. McCain missed the first rally in New Hampshire, the state where he had soundly beaten Bush, because of food poisoning from "a catfish and shrimp dinner" in Mississippi a day earlier, noted press accounts. Nonetheless, he rallied in Maine a day later following the third presidential debate and praised the Texas governor in person, calling Bush a man who was "fully prepared to assume the responsibilities" of the White House.

John McCain's words could have been a critical vote of confidence that swayed some of his own supporters to cast their lots for Bush. What no one knew a week before Election Day was just how critical every vote would be in the Bush versus Gore race.

In one of the closest presidential elections in U.S. history, Gore narrowly won the popular vote nationwide. But American presidents are actually selected by the electoral college, and a candidate wins a state's electors by winning the popular vote in that state—whether by a single vote or by millions of votes. By November 8, the day after Election Day, neither Bush nor Gore had locked up the required majority of electoral college votes because the popular vote in Florida had been too close to determine the winner. Only after a monthlong battle waged in the courts—including the Florida Supreme Court and the United States Supreme Court—would Bush be declared the winner, by a razor-thin margin, of the popular vote. With Florida's electoral votes in his column, Bush thus became the 43rd president of the United States.

If John McCain had been counting on an Al Gore victory to grant him another crack at the White House in 2004, his plans had been derailed. However, back during the primaries, one news columnist had noticed that McCain seemed happier after he lost elections than when he won, suggesting he actually felt nobler in defeat. Perhaps his run for the presidency was just the latest in a series of dramas where he played the heroic outsider, a sort of patron saint of lost causes.

It was an interesting bit of armchair psychology, supported to some degree by McCain's tours of duty at Episcopal High, Annapolis, Vietnam, and the U.S. House and Senate. Even campaign finance reform fit the mold. Few issues before the Senate were given less chance of succeeding, and yet McCain had been the perennial torchbearer.

But with the prominence he had garnered in the presidential race, John McCain was no longer just a rogue senator who challenged the establishment. He had become a crusader to be reckoned with. And suddenly, campaign finance reform, his Holy Grail, seemed within reach.

Favorable omens had begun appearing even before the general election. In June 2000, Senator McCain had managed to crack the wall erected by opponents to reform in the U.S. Senate. Powerful Republicans like Majority Leader Trent Lott had used every maneuver at their disposal to muzzle McCain's assaults on the status quo. But even he couldn't prevent McCain from finally winning a vote on legislation requiring full disclosure of contributors and spending by politically motivated groups who wanted to remain anonymous.

Such groups had been designated "527s" in the U.S. tax code. They included organizations like the Sierra Club, which frequently opposes what it considers assaults on the environment. However, another 527 called Republicans for Clean Air had taken advantage of loopholes in campaign finance laws to buy ads attacking John McCain's environmental record. The spots were run in early March during the Republican primaries, a tactic that helped to undermine his candidacy.

But McCain and his Democratic Senate ally Russ Feingold were the beneficiaries now, noted *CQ Weekly* in its June 10, 2000, issue. "McCain and Feingold predicted that their victory—a precision attack on a single area of the

McCain and Russell Feingold of Wisconsin speak at the U.S. Capitol about campaign finance reform, March 19, 2001. Within a few weeks, the two would see their bill—which they had introduced every year since 1995—finally approved by the Senate, 59-41.

law—could pressure colleagues to support their broader campaign finance goal: a complete ban on 'soft money,' the unlimited, unregulated cash that flows from corporations and labor unions to political parties."

CQ Weekly was right on the money. In July, Congress approved the 527 legislation and President Clinton signed it. It was one small step in the right direction for meaningful campaign finance reform.

But McCain showed that he wouldn't be content with this small step. And he demonstrated, once again, that he had the determination to wage a long fight. Soon after George W. Bush was sworn into office on January 17, the senator revealed his plan to reintroduce his campaign finance reform bill immediately—in order, he said, to get it out of the way before the president pursued his own legislative agenda. All eyes focused on the new president to see if he would use his influence to help McCain successfully shepherd reform through Congress.

"This is not McCain vs. Bush," the Arizona senator said on NBC's *Meet the Press* January 21. "I believe we can work together, but we know that delay is death." McCain was optimistic his bill would be considered soon after Congress convened—the sooner the better. Ultimately, however, McCain agreed—after meeting with President Bush—to wait a while before tackling campaign finance reform.

By March, the bruising battle over campaign finance reform was under way in the Senate. To the surprise of many, McCain and Feingold marshaled sufficient support to get their bill—also known as the Bipartisan Campaign Reform Act of 2001—passed by the Senate. The vote was 59-41. The act's central provision is a ban on soft money in federal elections.

In early July, the House of Representatives seemed poised to vote on similar legislation—called the Shays-Meehan bill—but procedural maneuvering by opponents blocked the vote. McCain vowed to keep up the fight for campaign reform, and many Washington observers seemed to feel that his side had a decent chance of prevailing.

If he does see his reform legislation pass Congress—and if President Bush doesn't veto it—what will John McCain turn his energies to next? He'll turn 68 in 2004, past prime for a presidential contender. Moreover, odds are he'd first have to beat President George W. Bush for the Republican nomination, an uphill battle if ever there was one.

For now, all that John McCain will hint is that 2004 seems like a good time to chart a new course in his epic odyssey. He told *Esquire* magazine, "I can see myself believing that eighteen years in the Senate is enough. If you can't accomplish what you want to accomplish in eighteen years, then you probably are not going to in six more years after that."

CHRONOLOGY

1936	John Sidney McCain born August 29 in the Panama Canal Zone
1954	Graduates from Episcopal High School, Virginia
1958	Graduates from U.S. Naval Academy, Annapolis, Maryland
1967	Survives explosions and fire aboard USS *Forrestal*; shot down in October on bombing mission over Hanoi, North Vietnam
1968	Admiral Jack McCain named Commander in Chief, Pacific; his son refuses North Vietnamese offer to go home ahead of other POWs
1969	North Vietnamese leader Ho Chi Minh dies; American POWs almost immediately treated better in prison camps
1971	Camp Unity POWs revolt over right to hold church services
1972	President Richard Nixon escalates bombing of North Vietnam
1973	U.S. and North Vietnam sign Paris Peace Accords; U.S. involvement in war ends, and POWs return home
1980	McCain divorces wife Carol; three months later, marries Cindy Hensley
1982	Wins two-year term to U.S. House of Representatives in First Congressional District, Phoenix, Arizona
1984	Wins reelection to House
1986	Wins one of Arizona's seats in the U.S. Senate
1989	Avoids censure in Senate for Keating Five scandal
1992	Reelected to U.S. Senate for second six-year term
1998	Reelected to U.S. Senate for third term
1999	Campaigns for Republican nomination for the presidency
2001	Helps get campaign finance reform legislation passed in the Senate

FURTHER READING

Brace, Ernest C. *A Code to Keep: The True Story of America's Longest-Held Civilian Prisoner of War in Vietnam.* New York: St. Martin's, 1988.

McCain, John S., and Mark Salter. *Faith of My Fathers.* New York: Random House, 1999.

Timberg, Robert. *The Nightingale's Song.* New York: Simon & Schuster, 1995.

Website

Straight Talk America. Straight Talk America PAC. Washington, D.C. *www.straighttalkamerica.com*

INDEX

PICTURE CREDITS

Page

2: Courtesy of Sen. John McCain's Office
3: Courtesy of the McCain Family
13: Courtesy of Sen. John McCain's Office
15: Courtesy of Sen. John McCain's Office
17: Courtesy of Sen. John McCain's Office
20: Courtesy of Sen. John McCain's Office
22: Courtesy of Sen. John McCain's Office
25: Courtesy of Sen. John McCain's Office
28: Courtesy of Sen. John McCain's Office
30: Courtesy of Sen. John McCain's Office
33: Courtesy of Sen. John McCain's Office
37: Associated Press, AP
40: Courtesy of Sen. John McCain's Office
43: Courtesy of Sen. John McCain's Office
46: Courtesy of Sen. John McCain's Office
50: Associated Press, AP
54: Courtesy of Sen. John McCain's Office
57: Courtesy of Sen. John McCain's Office
58: Bettmann/Corbis
61: Courtesy of Sen. John McCain's Office
64: Courtesy of Sen. John McCain's Office
65: Courtesy of Sen. John McCain's Office
66: Courtesy of Sen. John McCain's Office
68: Courtesy of Sen. John McCain's Office
72: Courtesy of Sen. John McCain's Office
75: Courtesy of Sen. John McCain's Office
76: Courtesy of Sen. John McCain's Office
78: Courtesy of Sen. John McCain's Office
83: Courtesy of Sen. John McCain's Office
85: Courtesy of Sen. John McCain's Office
88: Associated Press, AP
92: Associated Press, AP
95: © Reuters NewMedia Inc./Corbis
98: © Reuters NewMedia Inc./Corbis
100: Courtesy of Sen. John McCain's Office
103: © AFP/Corbis
105: Associated Press, AP
108: © Reuters NewMedia Inc./Corbis

Cover photos: Courtesy of Sen. John McCain's Office

Richard Kozar has written 11 Chelsea House books, including biographies of Hillary Rodham Clinton, Elizabeth Dole, and Michael J. Fox. He lives in Whitney, Pennsylvania, with his wife, Heidi, and daughters, Caty and Macy.

James Scott Brady serves on the board of trustees with the Center to Prevent Handgun Violence and is the vice chairman of the Brain Injury Foundation. Mr. Brady served as assistant to the President and White House press secretary under President Ronald Reagan. He was severely injured in an assassination attempt on the president, but remained the White House press secretary until the end of the administration. Since leaving the White House, Mr. Brady has lobbied for stronger gun laws. In November 1993, President Bill Clinton signed the Brady Bill, a national law requiring a waiting period on handgun purchases and a background check on buyers.